I0164048

# FROM
# Hinduism
## TO
# Christianity

## Embracing the Spiritual Journey

## ANJLI SHARMA

Copyright © 2020 by Anjli Sharma

All rights reserved. No part of this publication may be reproduced, stored in a retrieval system or transmitted in any form or by any means—electronic, mechanical, photocopy, recording or any other—except for brief quotations in printed reviews, without permission of the author.

Some of the names in this book have been changed to protect the privacy of the individuals involved.

All Scripture quotations, unless otherwise indicated, are taken from The Holy Bible, New International Version®, NIV®. Copyright © 1973, 1978, 1984, 2011 by Biblica, Inc. ™ Used by permission. All rights reserved worldwide.

Scripture quotations marked MSG are taken from The Message. Copyright © 1993, 1994, 1995, 1996, 2000, 2001, 2002. Used by permission of NavPress Publishing Group.

Scripture quotations marked NKJV are taken from the New King James Version. Copyright © 1979, 1980, 1982, by Thomas Nelson, Inc. Used by permission. All rights reserved.

Scripture quotations marked KJV are taken from the King James Version. Copyright © 1611, 1613, 1629, 1638, 1762, 1769 by Thomas Nelson, Inc. Used by permission. All rights reserved.

Scripture quotations marked NLT are taken from the Holy Bible, New Living Translation, copyright © 1996, 2004. Used by permission of Tyndale House Publishers, Inc., Wheaton, Illinois. All rights reserved.

Scripture quotations marked NASB are taken from the New American Standard Bible ®, Copyright © 1960, 1962, 1963, 1968, 1971, 1972, 1973, 1975, 1977, 1995 by the Lockman Foundation. Used by permission.

Scripture quotations marked ESV are taken from The ESV® Bible (The Holy Bible, English Standard Version®), copyright © 2001 by Crossway, a publishing ministry of Good News Publishers. Used by permission. All rights reserved.

Scripture quotations marked AMP are taken from the Amplified ® Bible. Copyright © 1954, 1958, 1962, 1964, 1965, 1987 by The Lockman Foundation. Used by permission.

Cover Design by 100Covers.com
Interior Design by FormattedBooks.com
Editors: Chauncey Alexander and Tina Pocernich

ISBN:.978-0-578-71596-4

# Dedication

I dedicate this book to God because He knows I like reading books. He preferred I write one. I was led by God to write this book.

Habakkuk 2:2 *Then the Lord replied: "Write down the revelation and make it plain on tablets so that a herald may run with it."*

Three words: It is finished!

.

# Introduction

Dear Amazing Reader,

Do you know you made a great choice in choosing to read this book? Perhaps you saw the title *From Hinduism to Christianity* and thought *Wow! That's a big change to go from one religion to another. How is that possible? Can that really happen to someone? Or to me? How does that happen? What is that like?*

You may have a lot of questions. *How can a person change their religion like that? Is that even possible?* The answer to these questions is *yes*, and if it happened to me, then I am one hundred percent certain it can happen for anyone—including you.

To be completely honest it's not about a change of religions, it's about a relationship change with a God who is *all* about *love*—a reconnecting with a God who knows everything about your past, present, and future.

Are you going through something you haven't told anyone about? Are you sick and tired of doing the same thing over and over and nothing changes? Are you going through a health issue that's tiring you out? Are you wondering, *what's my purpose in life*? In the world we live in, we find many different religions, crime rates increasing, violence everywhere, sex trafficking, homeless people on the streets, and broken people committing suicide.

Where is peace? You hear bad news every day on TV news stations, but you don't hear about people being free and finding peace from the items listed above. John 16:33 says *These things I have spoken to you, that in Me you may have peace. In the world you will have tribulation; but be of good cheer, I have overcome the world.* (NKJV) John 3:16-18 says *For this is how God loved the world: He gave his one and only Son, so that everyone who believes in him will not perish but have eternal life. God sent his Son into the world not to judge the world, but to save the world through him. There is no judgment against anyone who believes in him, but anyone who does not believe in him has already been judged for not believing in God's one and only Son.* (NLT) God loves the world and people, but He is displeased with sin, and people are slaves to sin in this world. He wants people to live in freedom.

It's really easy for human beings to mess up and struggle in our worries, fears, hurts, wounds, tension, stress, anxieties, and brokenness, but it's really hard for us to fix it by ourselves. Instead we survive with a smile on our faces to say to those around us *I am okay* while we live with a hurting heart. We have a God that loves us even in our mess-ups. We can turn and change our hurting hearts to healed hearts with Jesus as our healer.

Do you want to see change in your life like you've never experienced before? Do you want to know who God really is? Do you really want *true love* from an invisible God that cares deeply about you? Would you like to know what real Christianity is all about? I would highly encourage you to continue reading and see for yourself why you should know and go after Jesus Christ.

# CHAPTER 1

# My Testimony

I was born in 1987 in Augusta, Georgia. A year later, my father decided to move us to Norristown, Pennsylvania. After moving we settled into a low-income neighborhood. At the time my parents were struggling to find jobs to pay rent and bills. My dad studied to become a computer engineer and worked in the military, and my mother worked night shifts at the post office. I didn't like that she had to work night shift. It was a nightmare for me to see her go to work and leave me all alone with the imaginary monsters in my mind. When she found a babysitter for me, I would hide underneath the bed in order to avoid going to the babysitter's house. My mom and I were close emotionally. I was mommy's little girl and it was hard being away from her because of our close relationship.

When I was less than a year old a family member locked me in the bathroom and slapped both sides of my jaw until I bled. It angered my mom and uncle. We later learned it caused long-term, physical damage to my jaw. The police gave the family member a warning, and he spent one night in jail.

It wasn't until I was ten years old when my mom took me to the dentist that we found out the real damage to my jaw. I thought *this place is cool* it had a big red toothbrush outside the dentist office. I had never been to the dentist before. I remember sitting in the dentist chair and one dentist examined my teeth. After that ten more Indian dentists took turns examining and diagnosing my jaw. They told my mother and me, "She needs surgery."

We left the office and my mom said, "They are crazy," but we didn't understand why surgery was needed at the time. The next time I went to the dentist, I was seventeen years old. I had four wisdom teeth pulled out. After taking pain medications and antibiotics, I needed to see a specialist because the pain would not go away. This time it was a maxillofacial doctor. I was diagnosed with TMJ (temporomandibular joint dysfunction) which causes pain in your jaw joints and muscles. I didn't realize that what the family member did when I was so little was still affecting my jaw. Surgery was my only option—I had no choice. I suffered with TMJ throughout my childhood years due to the abuse of that family member. I felt hurt, rejected, angry, betrayed, and unforgiving toward that individual.

Growing up my parents had a lot of marriage problems —physical and emotional abuse, cheating, controlling, pride, greed, and manipulation—all led to them getting divorced. Their divorce made me feel hurt, isolated, unprotective, lonely, rebellious, and insecure. Without my father, I was missing love, protection, and security.

As an elementary school child, I was bullied in school, leaving me struggling with low self-esteem issues, not standing up for myself, and experiencing rejection from people. I started becoming more disobedient, prideful, insecure, and disrespectful to my parents.

When I was ten years old, my mom took me to a church to see the Mary and Joseph play. I remembered taking pictures with them and sitting near them. Someone in the church told me to pray before I eat and say the word *Amen*, so I prayed before I ate my food and said *Amen*. My response was open, accepting, and I did what I was told. That was my first experience in a traditional church. No one told me anything about Jesus or Christianity after that. It was completely unfamiliar to me.

As years went by, I followed my parents' Hinduism teachings, stories, and pujas (prayer gatherings and worship). As a Hindu, I was not allowed to eat beef because we worshipped cows, since they give us dairy food. I remembered watching a lot of movies about three hundred thirty million gods and reading books about them. Growing up I only knew five of them: Krishna the blue god; Brahma, the god with four heads; Ganesh the elephant god; Vishnu the snake god; and Hanuman the monkey god. What I saw and heard in the Indian culture and religion was all I knew and experienced growing up as a Hindu.

Growing up through the years before I became a Christian, my understanding of Christianity was backward. I thought it was all about exorcisms. I didn't have any other perspective by which to see Christianity, but I had watched horror films about a girl with a foamy mouth, twisted head and body, and an evil man's voice. I had the same horror mentality: people being delivered from demonic spirits, and priests using their cross to burn them. The horror movie perspective on Christianity made it look bad. It was something I never thought I'd believe in.

I also thought Christianity was for American white people only. I didn't think I was allowed to believe in this religion. I never knew about Jesus from films either, because they never talked about what he did for all humanity. However, I do remember watching the movie *The Passion of the Christ*. That movie literally made me cry. It was so deep. I highly encourage you to see it. It will move you to tears as you see what Jesus did on the cross.

When I was thirteen years old, I was playing kickball outside with boys from our apartment complex. My dad saw me playing with them, called me to come, and told me to not play with them. He was very overprotective. I didn't know why it was an issue for him because it was innocent play. I was not allowed to have an Indian, celebrity-crush poster in my room because he thought it would be a distraction from my studies. I was very upset when he took it down. I didn't see anything wrong with his being over-protective, because a father would do that for their child.

My rebellious years started when I turned fifteen. I wasn't confident in my appearance or how I dressed. I had a lot of self-image issues and insecurities. I was going through an identity crisis. I needed something to fill that missing space in my heart—it was a desperate cry for love.

Myspace was the website where I thought I found my soul mate. I saw a picture of an Indian boy named Manveer who I thought was attractive and decided to add him. I started falling in love with this boy who lived and grew up near where I lived. The relationship went from casual to deep. He visited almost every weekend. We saw each other on special occasions like birthday parties, dinners, graduation, and BBQs. We went to the beach together and amusement parks.

I was given a promise ring and we planned to get married after completing college. Our families were happy for us that we were together. They watched us grow together from late high school through college. I didn't have any knowledge at the time regarding relationships and marriage. My only knowledge was lust.

During the years at Montgomery County Community College we were struggling with our studies and relationship. While I dated him, I went through storms of misery. I was emotionally and physically abused, attempting suicide when he would leave or mistreat me through manipulation and control. We broke up and made up constantly. It was obstacle after obstacle going through the relationship rollercoaster. I wasn't allowed to go with anybody else and wouldn't anyway because I remained faithful to him. I had no way out of my dark bubble—it was the only choice I thought I had.

Four years later it finally happened. I was going through a lot of struggles in college. Then I saw my boyfriend post stuff on Facebook out of jealousy and it hurt me emotionally. That's when my boyfriend of four years, whom I thought would be my soul mate, whom I thought would marry and would spend the rest of my life with, broke up with me for good! There was no going back this time, I had no choice but to move forward which was extremely difficult. I thought, *Hey I was supposed to marry this guy who gave me a promise ring. Why?!* My heart broke into pieces and I went through the roller coaster emotions because of it. I felt worthless, like a nobody. I didn't know what to do. I was miserable and had no happiness. I thought *this is what life is like for the rest of my life.*

When I was twenty-five-years old I went to Harcum College to become a Radiologic Technician. I started really well in my classes, but as time went on, I was struggling with college, my mind, and my identity. One day at lunch I met a Suriname girl named Shamirah, whom I became fast friends with, in my first year of college. We were sitting across from each other in the lounge— both studying and eating. We started talking. There was something about her that I was really attracted to, it was *something different*. I was drawn to her peaceful and friendly personality. We became close friends right away.

One day, I was going to lunch, and I saw her with a guy friend. I wondered *Who is this guy?* and *Why was he sitting with her?* She introduced me to her new boyfriend Anthony, and he was very comical. Shamirah really liked him and they spent a lot of time together. They wanted to double date, so Anthony introduced me to one of his friends.

At the time I was desperate for love, so I looked for love from guys who brought disappointment after disappointment. I wanted to fall in love and stay in love. I went on date after date with guys until I found one guy who I was drawn to.

In January 2013, Anthony and Shamirah, Ruben my ex-boyfriend, Ricardo a military friend and I drove one weekend to bring Ricardo to the military base in Forth Braggs, North Carolina. We were partying, drinking, smoking weed, playing video games, and having a wild time. The second night Ruben and I were having problems and we weren't talking. I started crying and didn't know what to do. I felt like a dropped glass—shattered into pieces and all that was left was the shards.

I believe all the drinking, smoking weed, and emotional stress opened doors to demons. The next day, when I woke up, I heard Shamirah say some gruesome things, and I didn't understand what was happening. It was so out of character that I wondered *is this a joke*? Once we all woke up, we held her down. Anthony took her into the shower as if it was holy water to cast the spirits out. It took a long time for the spirit or spirits to leave her. Once she came out of the bathroom,

Anthony took her to the bedroom. Ricardo had been praying and reading the Bible to her. Shamirah looked at me while I was sitting on the floor doing yoga and said, "Anjii . . ."

My eyes opened wide, looking at her. Suddenly I felt a dark, invisible, evil presence come at me. My friends quickly came to pray over me to remove the evil spirit from me. I turned and banged the wall, then turned around to Ruben and Anthony and said in a demonic voice "Leave me alone!"

While looking at Anthony, the evil spirit shifted from me to him. We all had to hold him down for a long period of time. We poured water bottles on him like they were holy water, trying to get the evil spirits out. It was like the movie "*The Exorcism*". We were all very scared and didn't know what to do. We moved Anthony to the living room and his body was fighting with the spirit that was inside of him.

I didn't know what to do to free Anthony from the demons torturing him. With my eyes wide open, I stepped back watching all this happen, paused, and said three memorable words: "I accept Jesus!" Immediately the unseen dark spirits flew out of his body and banged against the window, which I saw physically happen. I didn't know where those words came from, but later realized they were from God. My friends had never talked about Jesus to me before this, but they were all caring, loving, considerate, and capable Christians.

Anthony, Ruben, Shamirah, and I drove back to Pennsylvania from North Carolina. I was confused about my beliefs and unsettled with what I experienced. I couldn't understand why this was happening. I was stuck in my emotions, worries, anxieties, and fears. We all prayed after we returned from North Carolina for protection from the demons following us, and we shared a time of confession and communion, even though I wasn't sure what that was.

While Anthony was under the power of the demon, he had a vision of being in hell. During communion, Anthony spoke to me more about what he saw in hell; he saw demons torturing people. He specifically saw a girl get tortured there. He said it felt like the two minutes he was there was way too long. He wanted to get out of there fast. He saw something that I never thought would happen.

I had a silver metal carved elephant Hindu god in my car. My parents told me to put it on my car dashboard, and worship and pray to it every day. Anthony saw this elephant god in hell and saw the demon dancing and worshipping around the elephant god—it called me her meat sack. He said it called me her meat sack because since I was living in sin at the time, she knew I would be in hell eventually. She was speaking of my future and what my role would be in hell. I was shocked and confused. It was hard to believe what I was hearing because I didn't fully understand what my friends were telling me.

I did what they told me to do in communion: we ate bread which symbolized Jesus's body broken for us on the cross, and drank wine symbolizing his blood poured out for us. He gave his body as a living sacrifice to forgive us of our sins completely. It is a remembrance and symbol of why he died on the cross for our sins and what he went through for us.

The next morning, Shamirah shared more about Christianity. She emailed me information from a website about becoming a new Christian. I wasn't really interested right then, because I was still in deep shock after everything we experienced.

Once I arrived home, I told my mom what happened. She didn't believe me at all. She asked, "Why did you go to North Carolina?" I thought later on if I hadn't gone, God may not have opened my eyes to the truth about the religion I was in.

He used that trip to show me how Satan the devil had blinded me. I probably wouldn't have seen the truth if I had not gone to North Carolina.

The truth of Jesus brought me freedom. It was hard standing my ground at the time because I didn't know what to do, what to say, or how to stand firm and strong in my faith in Christ. My faith was still so new, I wasn't even sure about all my own beliefs; I just knew I chose Jesus over the Hindu gods. My family came against me for believing in Jesus. They felt I was rebelling against them because I left their religion and accepted Jesus. I felt alone spiritually because I was the only one in the family going toward God's direction. They thought I was crazy and weird for being a Christian. I became the first—the only—Christian in the family.

The same night when we got back from North Carolina, Anthony and Shamirah called me and said, "Whatever you do, don't go in the basement." I wondered why not? Anthony said Shamirah had a dream that a demon was in my basement, laughing. I was very scared and stayed away from the basement.

I had nightmares that night of vague images of demon faces, so I didn't sleep well, and my mom could sense something was wrong. I asked Shamirah's father—a pastor—to pray for me for protection, and I invited God into my life so I could build a relationship with Him. After I prayed, my friends were happy for me saying, "We are victorious!" I still had mixed feelings; one side of me was shaken in my mind and heart from what happened in North Carolina. The other side was happy to have accepted Jesus because he brought me joy! I became hungry and thirsty to know more about the things of God. I *finally* gave up my religion for a relationship with God.

The next afternoon I saw this big light come from the sky—it looked as if angels were guarding and protecting the neighborhood. I didn't see angels, even though that would have been cool to see, but it looked like a light of victory shining down. I was still in a state of shock, thinking about everything that happened in the days previously.

That same month, Shamirah asked me to visit a church called In the Light Ministries in Philadelphia. The first time I went I was drawn to the lights, the music, the atmosphere, and the crowd of people. It looked like a club, but it was more like a Jesus club. The pastor preached. I had a lot of sin I was dealing with and felt led to obey every word I heard from him.

At this church, I felt *God's presence*—it was amazing. It was something I had *never* experienced before. I felt this overwhelming joy and peace. His presence gave me goosebumps and chills. It was like I was on cloud nine—Heaven. I wanted *more* of *God's presence* and became hungrier for Him. I was thirsting more for God and would get desperately upset if I didn't encounter His presence. I couldn't miss one Sunday *because* of *God's presence*! He was more important than religion. My love for God grew and grew. I became so joyful going to that church, and I didn't want to go back to the religion I was in before. I went from being a Hindu to now being a Christian. The more I went to church, the more I learned about God.

Before attending In the Light Ministries, I had a mentor that taught me about sin, forgiveness, baptism, Holy Spirit, and Calvary. I wanted my sins forgiven by God, so I asked Him for forgiveness. As time went on, I decided to get baptized. I wanted it to be God's timing and the opportunity came two days after my birthday. Baptism was the best birthday gift from God. After the process of believing, accepting, following God, and getting baptized in the Holy Spirit, life completely changed for me as I moved from old life to new life. Baptism is an outward public sign of that decision to turn from old life to new life.

I was driving from Collegeville to Philadelphia which took forty-five minutes with no traffic before church and one hour back with traffic every Sunday. My mom wasn't okay with me going to church. We got into a lot of heated debates about religion. I traveled anyway, I was so attracted to *God's presence*, it was hard to miss church. I went every Sunday for one year.

A little after one year, I felt God leading me to live in Philadelphia. In the Indian culture, parents expect their children to live with their parents until marriage to prevent financial struggles and provide protection. Because of the Indian culture, my parents had a fixed mindset of me living with them until moving out to get married. I felt it was *impossible* for me to move out on my own where I could grow, due to the cultural expectations.

Following God's leading, I did move from the suburbs to an unknown city—Philadelphia. I had never planned to move out, but God had other plans. Jeremiah 29:11 says, *"For I know the plans I have for you," says the Lord. "They are plans for good and not for disaster, to give you a future and a hope."* (NLT) God knows the future. You don't need psychics to tell you your future, because their source is from demonic powers giving false predictions. You would need true prophets who can speak into your future, because their source is from God.

I remember a time when I was really into astrology, horoscopes, and numerology to the point I made them my life. I would refer to them every time I needed to know about my future based on the stars, moon, and galaxy. If they didn't create you, how would they know your future?

Deuteronomy 18:10-12 says: *For example, never sacrifice your son or daughter as a burnt offering. And do not let your people practice fortune-telling, or use sorcery, or interpret omens, or engage in witchcraft, or cast spells, or function as mediums or psychics, or call forth the spirits of the dead. Anyone who does these things is detestable to the Lord. It is because the other nations have done these detestable things that the Lord your God will drive them out ahead of you.* (NLT)

All my life I was living a lie of deception. It was okay to worship handmade objects that look like us, but don't talk, see, or hear us. I worshipped those Hindu gods my whole life. I thought I was doing good by praying and worshipping them. Hearing my friend tell me about the elephant statue god that the demon was worshipping opened my eyes and made me see it *wasn't* a god to worship and pray to.

God says in His word:

> *This is what the Lord says—Israel's King and Redeemer, the Lord of Heaven's Armies: "I am the First and the Last; there is no other God. Who is like me? Let him step forward and prove to you his power. Let him do as I have done since ancient times when I established a people and explained its future. Do not tremble; do not be afraid. Did I not proclaim my purposes for you long ago? You are my witnesses— is there any other God? No! There is no other Rock—not one!"*
>
> *How foolish are those who manufacture idols. These prized objects are really worthless. The people who worship idols don't know this,*

*so they are all put to shame. Who but a fool would make his own god—an idol that cannot help him one bit? All who worship idols will be disgraced along with all these craftsmen—mere humans—who claim they can make a god. They may all stand together, but they will stand in terror and shame.*

*The blacksmith stands at his forge to make a sharp tool, pounding and shaping it with all his might. His work makes him hungry and weak. It makes him thirsty and faint. Then the wood-carver measures a block of wood and draws a pattern on it. He works with chisel and plane and carves it into a human figure. He gives it human beauty and puts it in a little shrine. He cuts down cedars; he selects the cypress and the oak; he plants the pine in the forest to be nourished by the rain. Then he uses part of the wood to make a fire. With it he warms himself and bakes his bread. Then—yes, it's true—he takes the rest of it and makes himself a god to worship! He makes an idol and bows down in front of it! He burns part of the tree to roast his meat and to keep himself warm. He says, "Ah, that fire feels good." Then he takes what's left and makes his god: a carved idol! He falls down in front of it, worshiping and praying to it. "Rescue me!" he says. "You are my god!"*

*Such stupidity and ignorance! Their eyes are closed, and they cannot see. Their minds are shut, and they cannot think. The person who made the idol never stops to reflect," Why, it's*

*just a block of wood! I burned half of it for heat
and used it to bake my bread and roast my meat.
How can the rest of it be a god? Should I bow
down to worship a piece of wood?" The poor,
deluded fool feeds on ashes. He trusts something
that can't help him at all. Yet he cannot bring
himself to ask, "Is this idol that I'm holding in
my hand a lie?"* Isaiah 44:6-20 (NLT)

When was the last time a Hindu god told you he loved you? Have you ever heard them speak? Have you ever felt their presence? Did they die for you? Did you ever hear any encouragement from those other gods telling you something about who you are to them? Are there any other gods out there in other religions that have spoken to you in a loud clear voice? God is a personal, intentional, and communicative God. I don't know about you, but I needed a God that was going to talk, love, and bring an inner transformation.

From religion to relationship. From gods to God. From bondage to freedom. Everyone has the right to choose. What you believe is what you become. What you choose determines what road you take. Where will you go? That is the question! See the table differences between Hinduism and Christianity noted below:

| HINDUISM | CHRISTIANITY |
|---|---|
| Believes in 330 million gods (multiple paths to god) | Believes in the Trinity (Father God, Son of God and Holy Spirit) One Bridge to God |

| Gives flowers and food to idols | Prays by bowing our heads and talking to God |
|---|---|
| No forgiveness of sins | God forgives past, present and future sins |
| Reincarnation into a species at next birth | Eternal Life with Jesus |
| Meditation by chanting the word Om | Meditation— Focusing on the word of God (Bible) that transforms your soul. |

# CHAPTER 2

# Relationship with Our Creator

## Who? What? Where? Why? How? Jesus.

God created this world before creating human beings. Then the first two human beings were created: Adam (man) and Eve (woman). They ran away from God because they listened to a lie from the devil that brought them shame and a disconnected relationship with God. They fell into the trap of sin that had a domino effect to every single human being. Our sin nature led us into brokenness of mind and heart. An endless cycle of sin without an understanding of how, why, where, what and who to escape. God had a plan in mind. He sent His son Jesus as a baby to save all people from their sins. John 3:16 *For God so loved the world, that he gave his one and only Son, that whoever believes in him shall not perish but have eternal life.*

The real question is why does God hate sin? Romans 6:23 *For the wages of sin is death…*When sin has control over your life, you live in it carrying misery, unhappiness, emptiness, and death. You'll recognize sin when you see crime rates increase; missing children on posters at Walmart; abortion clinics opening daily; spouses cheating, lying, and abusing their spouses; sexual trafficking on the streets; etc. Sin separates us from receiving the Spirit of God—His great real joy, peace, and love. You don't have to be afraid of sin, because you can be set free from it by the one and only Jesus. You can either live in sin or have Jesus destroy sin for you—if you let him. The choice is yours!

The shape of the cross is intersecting vertical and horizontal lines. The vertical line represents our connection with God. The horizontal line represents our connection with people.

The cross is where the punishment for *all* our sins was placed on Jesus. His hands and feet were pierced with nails holding him on the cross, hanging with his broken body and his blood spilled to take away all our sins. He defeated *all* darkness to bring *all* human beings into his light. He took away sin, death, and religion by allowing himself to be nailed to the cross. He went through the suffering of the cross just so he could set us free from suffering.

When the hour came for Jesus' body to die on the cross, He said three final words. They are recorded in John 19:30 *When Jesus had tasted it, he said, "It is finished!" Then he bowed his head and gave up his spirit.* (NLT)

> Romans 5:6-9 says *While we were still helpless [powerless to provide for our salvation], at the right time Christ died [as a substitute] for the ungodly. Now it is an extraordinary thing for one to willingly give his life even for an upright man, though perhaps for a good man [one*

*who is noble and selfless and worthy] someone might even dare to die. But God clearly shows and proves His own love for us, by the fact that while we were still sinners, Christ died for us. Therefore, since we have now been justified [declared free of the guilt of sin] by His blood, [how much more certain is it that] we will be saved from the wrath of God through Him.* (AMP)

When we were utterly helpless, Christ came at just the right time and died for us. Now, most people would not be willing to die for a murderer on the cross, though someone might perhaps be willing to die for a good person who does the right thing. However, Jesus died for each of us, whether we are the most evil person alive, or a good and decent person. Jesus' blood cleanses you from sin, and saves you from eternal hell, misery, and suffering.

Jesus' body was taken to the tomb and sealed in it. On the third day, Jesus' friend Mary Magdalene went to the tomb and saw the stone seal had already been rolled away. She went to go tell Jesus' closest friends, his disciples. Two followed her to the tomb and were shocked because his body was missing. After they returned to the others, Mary remained outside the tomb crying and saw two angels. John 20:13 says, *"Dear woman, why are you crying?" the angels asked her. "Because they have taken away my Lord," she replied, "and I don't know where they have put him" She turned to leave and saw someone standing there. It was Jesus, but she didn't recognize him.* (NLT)

Why would Jesus do all of this?

Good question. Simple answer: unexplainable love.

God can give us peace, joy, love, blessings, healing on the inside and the outside, and an abundant life. How do I know this? He says it in His word (the Bible) and He speaks to people's hearts to bring messages to bring signs of understanding and reveal Himself. Warning: God will chase after you whether you like it or not. He will pursue you because He desires to have a relationship with you. Exodus 20:4 says *"You must not make for yourself an idol of any kind or an image of anything in the heavens or on the earth or in the sea. You must not bow down to them or worship them, for I, the Lord your God, am a jealous God who will not tolerate your affection for any other gods."* (NLT) This scripture speaks life. He is not only God, but He is a Father to His people. God is jealous of you in a unique way; it's pure, honest, rich, and good. His *love* is deep, never-ending, and amazing. He does *not* want any person to be broken-hearted, hurt, addicted, lost, confused, miserable, fearful, blind, or hated because God created us out of love to love people and Him. He is jealous for us because he *loves* us and *wants* us completely!

When I was a Hindu, I never heard anyone talk to me about who Jesus was and what he could do for me. After accepting and finding Jesus, I learned a lot from my Christian friends about who Jesus is. He loved me when I was a sinner and he still loves me today. Where there is *love*, there is *life*! God breathes into my life, and that brings a life of freedom. He is not only God, but He is a Father to His people. He loves us so much that He wants an authentic relationship with each and every person in the world. He created people to be sons and daughters to Him.

Dear reader, I want to encourage you—no matter where you are, what you are doing, what you look or sound like, or what background, culture. or family you came from. Be encouraged by every word written in this book because God *loves you* no matter *what* you say or do. How do I know the love of God? When God changed me, it was because of His love for me. If it happened to me, then nothing is impossible for God to make it happen for *you*.

God is a God specializing in making a somebody out of a person who feels that they are not worthy or are a nobody. All the years when I was a Hindu, not once did I hear any Hindu tell me who Jesus was, nor did I hear them say Jesus is in our Hindu Bible, because nobody knows who Jesus is. I was a lost soul with a broken heart trying to find someone and something to fill up that empty space inside me. The worst part about it was I couldn't find Jesus in my religion. Hinduism is a Polynesian (many) religion. When you think about it, why is it that each god represents one element in the world, like the god of fertility, prosperity, wisdom, destruction, snake, elephant, etc., when in reality, one God *is* everything? I am not one to criticize the religion I was in, but I am here to say that I got *out* of it and converted into Christianity because I found *real* joy, love, and peace from God.

We all are created differently, even our hearts—not the physical, blood-pumping organs, but I mean heart as the deep, inner, emotional center of our beings. Whatever kind of heart you have, God knows it because He created you. It's one thing to put on a smiley face all day long to people, but it's another thing to have a hurting heart inside that no one knows about except God. What kind of heart do you want God to give you? Would you allow Him to give you a strong golden heart?

After choosing to follow Jesus Christ, God took me into a process of humbling my heart, restoring and healing my heart from past hurts, and bringing me into a spirit of humility. I went through a difficult process of being set free from pride that only God could do. I went through it one day at a time with God. There are ways to tell God about those deep dark secrets you have inside that you can't tell anybody else about. You can release your heart today to God without any judgement! I encourage you to try the following steps in developing a healthy heart, mind, and soul. Take out a pen and a blank piece of paper. Write out your responses to step one below, then in step two read them *out loud*—that part is *very* important. *Don't be afraid!* Be encouraged and get your freedom back today![1]

1.  Admit what has been bothering your mind and your heart. Write out all the mistakes, worries, fears, hatred, insecurities, pride, greed, envy, hurts, pain, lust, negative thoughts, and anything else from which you want God to set you free. There is nothing to be ashamed of, they are things to release from your heart.
2.  Say I confess, repent, and renounce each one by speaking them out loud privately.
3.  Turn the paper sideways and write the scripture 1 John 1:9 over those sins you listed.

    John 1:9 says, *If we confess our sins, He is faithful and just to forgive us our sins and to cleanse us from all unrighteousness.* (NKJV)

4.  Tear that paper up into pieces to get the peace that can only be found in *Jesus.* Please note: you can also flush your dark past down the toilet, burn it up in a bonfire, or throw it in the trashcan. The freedom is yours!

    *After this presentation to Israel's leaders, Moses and Aaron went and spoke to Pharaoh. They told him, "This is what the Lord, the God of*

*Israel, says: Let my people go so they may hold a festival in my honor in the wilderness."*

*"Is that so?" retorted Pharaoh. "And who is the Lord? Why should I listen to him and let Israel go? I don't know the Lord, and I will not let Israel go."*

*But Aaron and Moses persisted. "The God of the Hebrews has met with us," they declared. "So let us take a three-day journey into the wilderness so we can offer sacrifices to the Lord our God. If we don't, he will kill us with a plague or with the sword."*

*Pharaoh replied, "Moses and Aaron, why are you distracting the people from their tasks? Get back to work! Look there are many of your people in the land, and you are stopping them from their work."* Exodus 5:1-5 (NLT)

In this true story God sent Moses and Aaron to speak to Pharaoh about letting the slaved Israelites go so they could follow God, but Pharaoh was disobedient to God's order. God had no choice but to send ten increasingly awful plagues to force Pharaoh to release the Israelites to be free to worship the Lord and be healthy. Just like how Pharaoh's heart was hardened by not listening and being disobedient to the commandment God gave, our hearts can be hardened also when we don't obey God's directive to forgive, but live in bitterness which can affect our heart and other systems in our body causing diseases and sickness. Exodus 23:25 says *"You must serve only the Lord your God. If you do, I will bless you with food and water, and I will protect you from illness."* (NLT)

God wants us to use wisdom in going to psychologists, therapists, doctors, and counselors to find healing. They can help in restoring our health, but can they heal us permanently physically, emotionally, or spiritually? You would have to keep paying doctors to find out what's wrong with you. God can lighten your health—all it takes is to humbly ask God for healing. It's okay to ask Jesus, who is the great physician. There is nothing impossible for God to heal.

When the power of God comes upon you, your hands can be used to touch a person in pain, and when we pray for that person, God takes over and heals them completely. Once my dad was working and my co-workers told him, "Your daughter prayed for me and my legs got healed." He couldn't believe it. It was a shock to him! Another time I approached a coworker and saw she had a brace on her right arm. I asked her, "Can I pray for you?" She agreed, so I prayed for her and went back home.

The next day when I saw her, she said, "I don't have the brace—God healed through you." God is the *only* healer. She didn't need the brace any longer and she was able to shred papers in the shred bin with ease.

The only bridge that connects *you* to God is Jesus Christ. In John 14:6 *Jesus answered, "I am the way and the truth and the life. No one comes to the Father except through me."* Anybody can believe in God, but not everybody can believe in Jesus, which means not everyone is living in freedom from their past pains and hurts.

God wants *you*! He wants to be in a relationship with *you*! It's an open invitation to His presence. You can encounter His presence today by shouting out the name of *Jesus*! It will definitely put a smile on God's face. His heart will be pleased.

Below is a table showing some of the differences between a religion and a relationship with God. See following table:

| Religion with God | Relationship with God |
|---|---|
| Following man-made laws, rules, and rituals | Following God's Voice and the Ten Commandments |
| Attending only once-a-week gatherings out of a religious ritual | Seven days a week of spending time with God |
| Actions don't match with words | Actions do match up with words |
| Pointing out of wrongs to a person out of an impure heart | Correcting, helping, and leading a person to the right direction out of a loving heart |

There are so many different things in many religions people must do in order to please the gods they worship. God standards of instructions for us consist of only ten commandments. According to Exodus 20:3-17:

1. *No other gods, only me.*
2. *No carved gods of any size, shape, or form of anything whatever, whether of things that fly or walk or swim. Don't bow down to them and don't serve them because I am GOD, your God, and I'm a most jealous God, punishing the children for any sins their parents pass on to*

*them to the third, and yes, even to the fourth generation of those who hate me. But I'm unswervingly loyal to the thousands who love me and keep my commandments.*

3. *"No using the name of GOD, your God, in curses or silly banter; GOD won't put up with the irreverent use of his name.*

4. *Observe the Sabbath day, to keep it holy. Work six days and do everything you need to do. But the seventh day is a Sabbath to GOD, your God. Don't do any work—not you, nor your son, nor your daughter, nor your servant, nor your maid, nor your animals, not even the foreign guest visiting in your town. For in six days GOD made Heaven, Earth, and sea, and everything in them; he rested on the seventh day. Therefore GOD blessed the Sabbath day; he set it apart as a holy day.*

5. *Honor your father and mother so that you'll live a long time in the land that GOD, your God, is giving you.*

6. *No murder.*

7. *No adultery.*

8. *No stealing.*

9. *No lies about your neighbor.*

10. *No lusting after your neighbor's house—or wife or servant or maid or ox or donkey. Don't set your heart on anything that is your neighbor's.* (MSG)

Even with only ten, these are impossible for anybody to follow and we see this is currently what's happening in our world. Everybody is breaking these commandments left and right. It's easy to follow man-made laws that oppose what God has said. The commandments apply to people who believe and follow God. When we sin, we can come to Jesus to forgive us for breaking God's commandments. God truly wants repentance from people.

Christianity is not the amount of time you spend, it's how you spend your time to honor God. Jesus says you don't have to do all of that to please me, I have already paid the price by shedding my blood. I have pleased the Father, so that you my daughter and you my son can have a relationship with me. That's how much God loves us. We don't need to do a bunch of things to please God, it only takes one choice—accept freedom we find in God or accept misery, depression, fears, hate, and torture. That was the purpose of Jesus dying on the cross for every single human being on this planet.

Jesus lived and died and is alive today for every single albino, Asian, black, blue, Chinese, Filipino, French, German, Indian, Italian, Korean, Mexican, Muslim, orange, pink, Persian, Puerto Rican, red, Russian, yellow, and white person. It doesn't matter what color your skin is because there is no racism, discrimination, nor prejudice in Heaven. Heaven celebrates faces of all colors. God sees the intentions, actions, and motives of your heart rather than your outside appearance. When you look at yourself in the mirror, tell yourself these life-speaking words: *I see that I am created by God—fearfully and wonderfully made. I am a beautiful reflection of God. I am a strong person that can and will conquer all things through Christ who gives me strength.* When we allow the Holy Spirit, who is God that fits inside of me, into our souls, we can *really* become positive and encouraging to people.

Our hearts need to be refined, corrected, molded, cleansed, and purified with God first. When our hearts are set right with God, then our hearts can be made right with people. Warning: Jesus may cause extreme happiness that will bring you endless joy. Being in a relationship with God is the *best* decision to make! It's an unregrettable decision. It's what God desires for His entire creation.

The three most important keys to unlocking God's heart are obedience, intimacy, and faith. Obeying God is doing what He tells you to do immediately or waiting to do it on His timing. It's that still small voice you hear inside of you. John 14:15 says, *"If you love me, **obey** my commandments."* (NLT, emphasis mine.) According to *Supernatural Deliverance*[2], by Guillermo Maldonado, "A hindered blessing does not change God's unconditional love for us, but obedience is the foundational kingdom principle for receiving His blessing. If you are rebellious and disobedient, you are acting according to the sinful nature, which is cursed; consequently, God's blessing cannot flow in your life." Surrendering your life to Jesus means repenting of the sinful ways of rebellion, disobedience, dishonor, and any other issue you may be going through. Surrender brings *freedom*. Do you want freedom today?

## Obedience = Blessings   Disobedience = Curses

One time I heard God speak to me in His audible voice. He said, "You must tell your Family about me! You must!" It was very authoritative. It sounded like a father telling his daughter to do an important assignment. As I heard His voice, my eyes opened wide because I was shocked He spoke to me. His voice was beautiful, and I wanted to hear it over and over again. It took my breath away. I told my family all at one time through a Facebook message. My obedience wasn't immediate because I didn't know it had to be quick. Obeying God is taking the action when directed to avoid the consequences of disobedience.

Other times when God told me to pray for someone, I went up to the person and asked, "Can I pray for you?" Every time they said yes!

My friend and I frequently went up to one person after another when we were out in public, whether at church, a mall, a yogurt store, or a dollar store, and as the Holy Spirit led us, we would ask if we could pray for them. One time I heard Holy Spirit say to me, *pray for her* (the woman in a couple), so I went up to my friend and said, "We've got to pray for her." We approached the couple and asked if we could pray for them. My friend shared her visions about them that were related to their current situation. They were blessed by and thankful for that.

We learn to pray for people inside the church but praying for people outside of church is stepping out of our comfort zone. When God tells you to do something, I highly encourage you to go for it! It pleases God's heart. For example, if He tells you to pray for someone, give ten dollars, hug someone, make a sandwich, do the dishes, pray for a specific person or nation, it's best to be obedient. God can say anything at any time. It's the littlest blessings that count. You won't regret it—you will reap it. Obeying the Spirit of God by listening to His voice brings joy and blessings.

Being intimate with God means building a close relationship; like a close friend you would talk to. The more you spend time with this person, the more you get to know what their heart is like. This is called intimacy. Like a friend to a friend, there can be intimacy between a human being and God as well. Intimacy does not mean sex, it means to develop a close relationship.

We can ask Him questions like *God what should I wear? What do you recommend I eat? What kind of hairstyle would you like? Should I buy this item? What do you have in mind for the day today?* It's okay to ask God tough questions to lead you to make the right decisions. It's important God leads us into the answers to our questions. He will never lead us wrong. God searches our hearts and finds things that bother us, make us happy, or sad. He sees what we think, what we are going to say, and a lot more than you know about yourself because God created you.

God wants us to spend time with Him by talking to Him. There's no right or wrong way to talk to God, because you're speaking to Him about how you feel. Talk to Him like He's your friend—it will be worth the time. When you talk to God, stay motionless and silent by getting quiet in your mind and heart to hear what He says about you. Whatever time you have, time with Jesus is where you can find, seek, know, listen, have fun, laugh, and enjoy him. Every second, hour and minute with God is worth spending. How will you use your time?

There are a lot of things in this world getting our attention and distracting us. Are there things like money, cars, jobs, problems, struggles, or a person in your life that you put first before the Spirit of God? We may not realize or recognize we are struggling in the things of this world such as pornography, gossip, fear, worries about finances, or pride because our minds are wired to this world and it's *normal*. What comes first in your life every day when you wake up in the morning?

Carved idols are not the only idols we need to consider, because we can put anything before God. We run to our firsts as our morning breakfast, such as social media, our girlfriend or boyfriend, yoga, exercise, TV, food, etc. No Judgement Zone here, so take a moment to name that one thing you know you go to first thing in the morning: _____. These things distract and take our focus away from God.

Early in the morning we must put God first before anything else over every area of our lives. We start the day right praying to God and staying with God. God is our first—we should come running fast toward Him instead of running away. The only way we can be more joyful, peaceful, and loving—to ourselves and other people—is by spending time with Jesus. Investing in your time behind closed doors with God is what He really wants. Quality over quantity. It doesn't matter how many hours it takes, what matters is what you're being filled up with when you're in the presence of God.

Worshiping God daily is a fighting weapon against the devil who is the enemy. Play any Christian worship song on YouTube that builds your love for God. What you hear, listen to, and see feeds your soul and spirit. Listening to cursing, depressing, and/or break up songs can build a negative mind and heart. It's important to be careful what we listen to. What have you been listening to on the radio lately? Is it helping or hurting your heart?

Our eyes are open to seeing the chaos in the news or magazines, and on television. Although we see the chaos happening, what Christians do is pray in Jesus name for God to bring peace, joy, protection, healing, guidance, and His wisdom to people who need it—for God to make the world a better place.

The Bible is also known as the word of God. Reading the word of God transforms your mind and heart. It is also used as a weapon of truth against the lies the devil says. There were times I was listening and believing in the lies of the enemy, but the truth is, my real identity is found in Jesus Christ. Truth is God says in the Bible we are heirs of Christ which means we are a royal people. When we begin to read the Bible over and over again, we get filled up until our bellies are full of rivers of living water. I guarantee you will be filled up with the joy that comes from the Lord. In joy, you will be jumping up and down and doing cartwheels. Joy is an exciting and contagious feeling that should spread like wildfire.

Faith grows when we choose to believe, as well as the reverse. Our belief grows when we choose faith. Then the more we see God's hand at work, the more faith we have built up, the greater our belief is as we go into new situations. Matthew 17:20 says "*. . . Truly I tell you, if you have faith as small as a mustard seed, you can say to this mountain, 'Move from here to there, and it will move. Nothing will be impossible for you.*"If we speak life to our situations such as *I am healed and free from darkness*, then it *will* happen! But if we say things like, *that's never going to happen, I'm broke, it's too hard, I can't do this*— then we speak death into our situations. Proverbs 18:21 says *Death and life are in the power of the tongue, and those who love it will eat its fruit.* (NKJV) Let's choose to speak more words of life into every difficult situation we face. Choose wisely the words you use.

Small faith (believe it) = anything is possible

Nothing happens in one day—there's a process that takes place like a child growing. It can take days, months, or years for spiritual growth to take place in our walk with Christ.

## Hearing God's Voice = Intimacy Is Developed

There is only one way to please God and that is through Jesus Christ. Why? There are a lot of different religions in the world that believe in God, but not every religion believes in Jesus. Jesus provides the salvation people need. Acts 4:12 states *And there is salvation in no one else, for there is no other name under heaven that has been given among men by which we must be saved.* (NASB) Anybody can be a good person but can still lie, cheat, or steal—which is sin. Accepting Jesus is accepting freedom from lying, cheating, and stealing.

When I was a Hindu, I always saw Christianity as another religion. What I did not know was it was actually a relationship with God. I didn't know I could have a relationship with a God I could trust. It changed my entire perspective positively. I experience His love by building an intimate relationship with Him. The Trinity (Tri = three and Unity = one) is three in one: The Father, the Son, and the Holy Spirit. The Father is God, the Son is Jesus, and the Holy Spirit is God's Spirit. According to 1 Timothy 2:5-6 *For there is one God and one Mediator who can reconcile God and humanity—the man Christ Jesus. He gave his life to purchase freedom for everyone.* (NLT) Jesus is a physical form of God. Holy Spirit is the invisible spirit of God—another form of God that can live inside of us (if we let Him) to lead us into the right direction in this dark world.

The Holy Spirit living in us guides, comforts, teaches, speaks, leads, casts out demons, encourages, convicts of sin, calms, counsels, helps, cleanses, and kills your sin. John 14:26 *But the Comforter, which is the Holy Ghost, whom the Father will send in my name, he shall teach you all things, and bring all things to your remembrance, whatsoever I have said unto you.* (KJV).

God sent the Holy Spirit to restore, heal, and bring us life. He loves you that much! Can you believe it? YES! It's the truth, and the truth will set you free. According to Galatians 5:22-23 *But the Holy Spirit produces this kind of fruit in our lives: love, joy, peace, patience, kindness, goodness, faithfulness, gentleness, and self-control. There is no law against these things!* (NLT) Be open to allowing God to develop your character in the process. It's God's fruitful characteristics of love, joy, peace, patience, kindness, self-control, faithfulness and gentleness that can flow through us as we become more like Him.

## The Fruit of the Spirit = Produces Character

Once we accept and receive the Spirit of God in our hearts, minds, and souls, we begin to be directed by the Holy Spirit to walk in freedom. When the Holy Spirit lives inside of our bodies, he feels what you feel and hears what you think. The Holy Spirit living inside of you protects you from all sickness and disease. When I was a Hindu, I was more religious than relational with God. I followed rules and regulations to please God.

According to Colossians 2:20-23 *If you have died with Christ to the elementary principles of the world, why, as if you were still living in the world, do you submit to rules and regulations, such as, "Do not handle [this], do not taste [that], do not [even] touch!"? (these things all perish with use)—in accordance with the commandments and teachings of men. These practices indeed have the appearance [that popularly passes as that] of wisdom in self-made religion and mock humility and severe treatment of the body (asceticism), but are of no value against sinful indulgence [because they do not honor God].* (AMP) Many people don't think they need Jesus because they are depending on following man-made rules of behavior to please the god of their world.

We are in a war between our spirit and our flesh. It's a daily battle for the winning of our souls. It's like a tug of war rope—pulled from two opposite directions. On one side there's the devil pulling us toward him and the other side where God is pulling us closer toward Him. The Holy Spirit living inside us pleases God, but the flesh we fight against pleases the devil.

Our flesh desires the things of this world such as sexual immorality, lust, sensuality, cheating, lying, jealousy, selfishness, idolatry, stealing, greed, and other worldly things. We can easily fall into a sinful trap when we follow our emotions, will, mind, and desires. We also can be tempted into something we don't want to do. Temptation to sin is *not* sin but giving in to the temptation to sin *is* sin. We are not perfect because we can and do make mistakes, but through those mistakes we can learn and grow from them to hopefully not repeat them. Mistakes don't define who we are.

When we receive the power of God in our hearts, God sees Jesus in us as righteous—perfect without any blemish, spot, stain, wrinkle of sin. Jesus Christ came to earth two thousand years ago not as a statue but as a real person who walked on this earth with his twelve closest friends and did life together with messed up people like us. He started a ministry, died on the cross to forgive *all* human beings of their sins permanently. Now you're probably wondering *why would a man die on the cross for me? What was the purpose of that?* Let me elaborate more on many different reasons. Let me start from the beginning of creation, according to what the Bible says.

The first chapter in the book of Genesis is the account of creation. Genesis 1:1 *In the beginning God created the heavens and the earth.* (NLT) Genesis 1:26-27 *Then God said, "Let us make human beings, in our image to be like us. They will reign over the fish in the sea, the birds in the sky, the livestock, all the wild animals on the earth, and the small animals that scurry along the ground. So, God created human beings in his own image. In the image of God, he created them; male and female he created them.* (NLT) The two human beings that God created were named Adam and Eve.

Genesis 1:28 continues *Then God blessed them and said, "Be fruitful and multiply. Fill the earth and govern it. Reign over the fish in the sea, the birds in the sky, and all the animals that scurry along the ground"* (NLT). We see here that God created human beings—it wasn't a human being that created a carved statue to worship. God created human beings to worship Him—*we* were created to worship Him. But Adam and Eve both fell into sin.

According to Genesis 3:1-6:

> *The serpent was the shrewdest of all the wild animals the Lord God had made. One day he asked the woman, "Did God really say you must not eat the fruit from any of the trees in the garden?"*
>
> *"Of course we may eat fruit from the trees in the garden,". the woman replied. "It's only the fruit from the tree in the middle of the garden that we are not allowed to eat. God said, 'You must not eat it or even touch it; if you do, you will die.'"*
>
> *"You won't die!" the serpent replied to the woman. "God knows that your eyes will be opened, as soon as you eat it, and you will be like God, knowing both good and evil." The woman was convinced.* (NLT)

Eve heard and believed what the serpent (who was the devil) said to her and fell into sin which broke the bridge between God and her. God warned her to protect and care for His creation. It's the same way today: we can hear negative thoughts that are *actually* lies and can easily fall into believing and accepting them. We get into having a long discussion with the devil and fall into believing the lies.

Genesis 3:6 *She saw that the tree was beautiful and its fruit looked delicious, and she wanted the wisdom it would give her. So she took some of the fruit and ate it. Then she gave some to her husband, who was with her, and he ate it, too. At that moment their eyes were opened, and they suddenly felt shame at their nakedness. So they sewed fig leaves together to cover themselves.* (NLT) This is where Adam and Eve felt shame and guilt for eating the rotten fruit from the tree after listening to the serpent that it was good for them, when God really said *You may freely eat the fruit of every tree in the garden—except the tree of the knowledge of good and evil. If you eat its fruit, you are sure to die.*" (Genesis 2:16) God gave us a choice—choose our will or His will over our lives. The devil can show you what looks good on the outside and lead you into a deceptive invitation. When you agree with his offer, that's when you fall into sin. Choosing God's way leads you to a life of freedom, love, peace, joy, and blessing. Choose wisely today.

Disobedience to God is sin; we were led by a deceiver telling us what God never said. From the time the fall of man took place, it has been passed down from one generation to another. Please note Satan is very cunning. According to the New Living Translation Study Bible[3], Satan will give you the Five Ds: Doubt, Discouragement, Diversion, Defeat, and Delay.

- Doubt to question God's word and His goodness.
- Discouragement that will make you look at your problems rather than at God.

- Diversion that makes the wrong things seem attractive—attention-grabbing so you will want them more than the right things.
- Defeat that will make you feel like a failure so that you don't even try.
- Delay that makes you put off doing something so that it never gets done.

After Adam and Eve both sinned, they felt guilty and embarrassed over their nakedness. They used fig leaves to cover their naked bodies. They were hiding their shame and guilt from God and couldn't face him. Sin caused a broken relationship with God. It separated human beings from God. God did not intend for that to happen, and the truth is God wants a relationship with *every* single human being because He created *every* single human being whom He loves deeply. God loves us unconditionally and longs to fellowship with us. Sin is the only thing that separates us from God, which is why God sent *his only begotten son, so that whoever believes in him shall not perish but have everlasting life* John 3:16.

Jesus died on the cross so you can have a righteous (free from sin) relationship with our Father in Heaven—God. Jesus is the son of God who came to Earth to save all human beings from sin. Jesus is powerful and he is a victor over sin. People understand and do various works based on their religious beliefs to try to earn God's approval. However, Jesus took the need for all that striving or working away by his death on the cross so he could have a relationship with his people. It's your choice to accept or reject.

Won't you come to Jesus and bring all your hurts, pain, suffering, worries, fears, and struggles? It didn't make sense to me in the beginning, but during the process it became clear to me. God knows our needs, desires, and wants. He knows how we think, what we think about, our every move, and even our pre-thinking (before we consciously thought about something). The question is do we trust in the truth of what He says? God has a bright future for us and can take us to places we've never even dreamed or thought.

There are approximately four thousand, two hundred religions[4] in the world, and one thing they all have in common is man-made teachings. I remembered my dad saying to me, "When you're born a Hindu you stay a Hindu." God says in Romans 3:23 *For **all** have sinned and fall short of the glory of God.* (NIV, emphasis mine.) and in Romans 5:8 *But God showed his great love for us by sending Christ to die for us **while** we were still sinners.* (NLT, emphasis mine.) Everyone is born a sinner regardless of their religion, race, background, or culture. The truth is we need Jesus no matter who we are twenty-four hours a day, seven days a week.

God wants to protect you from the cost of sin and has provided the means to do so. God is pleased with His son Jesus whom we can trust in because He is the God of truth. If you repent, believe, and accept Jesus today, you will be saved from going to hell consisting of eternal torture of your soul.

God is the Great Physician. He can heal any sickness or illness in existence. You can be free from visiting of porn websites, numerous sessions with your psychologist or counselor, hospitalization or medication for mental illness, partying at clubs, premarital sex (fornication), religious mindsets (a bunch of dos and don'ts), hospitalization, bars, haunted houses, watching horror movies like Paranormal Activity, playing the Ouija board that can wake up demonic spirits, and spending money on psychics when only God knows about your future. As a Hindu I had experienced some of the items listed above.

These are open doors to demons who want to steal, kill, and destroy your mind, body, and soul. John 10:10 says *The thief comes only to steal and kill and destroy; I have come that they may have life, and have it to the full.* There is a God that doesn't want us destroyed—He wants us to experience life. The thief is a reference to Satan or a demon. I once heard about a lady walking outside, leaving the church, and a thief came and stole her purse. Immediately she said the words, "Stop in the name of Jesus!" He dropped the purse and ran off.

Thieves and robbers are controlled by Satan the devil who assigns his demons to destroy people. The items I mentioned are territories ruled by demonic powers and influences in the world where we live. It's sad, but true. We can't see them through our natural eyes, but we can see them through spiritual eyes.

Who is Satan? Satan was originally created as a beautiful angel named Lucifer who worshiped God in Heaven. God sent a message to Satan through a prophecy regarding the death of the king of Tyre, according to Ezekiel 28:12-19: *Son of man, sing this funeral song for the king of Tyre. Give him this message from the Sovereign Lord: You were the model of perfection, full of wisdom and exquisite in beauty. You were in Eden, the garden of God. Your clothing was adorned with every precious stone—red carnelian, pale-green peridot, white moonstone, blue-green beryl, onyx, green jasper, blue lapis lazuli, turquoise, and emerald—all beautifully crafted for you and set in the finest gold. They were given to you on the day you were created. I ordained and anointed you as the mighty angelic guardian. You had access to the holy mountain of God and walked among the stones of fire. You were blameless in all you did from the day you were created until the day evil was found in you. Your rich commerce led you to violence, and you sinned. So I banished you in disgrace from the mountain of God. I expelled you, O mighty guardian, from your place among the stones of fire. Your heart was filled with pride because of all your beauty. Your wisdom was corrupted by your love of splendor. So I threw you to the ground and exposed you to the curious gaze of kings. You defiled your sanctuaries with your many sins and your dishonest trade. So I brought fire out from within you, and it consumed you. I reduced you to ashes on the ground in the sight of all who were watching. All who knew you are appalled at your fate. You have come to a terrible end, and you will exist no more.* (NLT)

What a beautiful beginning but an ugly ending. Long story short—Lucifer was a high-ranking guardian angel whose role was to protect God's holiness and lead the heavenly host of angels in worshipping God. As the passage said, he became filled with pride and was jealous of God's supernatural power. When he tried to supersede God and direct worship toward himself, he was kicked out of heaven. He became a fallen angel, now known as the devil, who will ultimately be cast into a pit of fire where there is total darkness. Hell is where the devil wants people to go because he still desires worship. He still wants to supersede God and take that worship for himself. But God did not create you for hell. He created you to be with Him and his son Jesus in heaven eternally.

If you were to die today, do you know where you would go? Satan is full of sin, *but* Jesus can take away *all* sin. The forgiveness Jesus can provide will seal you like a permanent tattoo—it will never come off. Why? So you can receive *freedom* from *all* depression, sadness, grief, isolation, anger, anxiety, fear, worry, lust, hatred, jealousy, irritation, annoyance, revenge, unforgiveness, bitterness, and if you have or know any other dark human emotion, please fill in the blank _____.

According to Matthew 7:13-14 Jesus says *"You can enter God's Kingdom only through the narrow gate. The highway to hell is broad, and its gate is wide for the many who choose that way. But the gateway to life is very narrow and the road is difficult, and only a few ever find it."* (NLT) Jesus is saying that there are two different paths. Many people take the shortcut which is the broad pathway because it's easier, faster, and everyone can do their own thing. It's easy for people to believe in other religions. It's easy to join the crowd with other people who are in the same boat—loving each other's misery and pretending life is okay.

The narrow path is harder and not as obvious. It is available for those seeking the truth. But it's hard to go a different direction where you're not like most people. Instead you choose a lifestyle where you no longer love misery, but you love people despite their misery.

People operate out of love or hate, light or darkness, obedience or disobedience, humility or pride, faith or fear, relationship or religion. It's our choice to make. The world will tell you who you are when you are living in the darkness. God expels the darkness by His light and reveals your identity in Jesus Christ. Jesus is the light of the world that penetrates all evil. There is not a single ounce of darkness in him. He is *completely light.*

Psalm 27:1 says *The Lord is my light and my salvation—so why should I be afraid? The Lord is my fortress, protecting me from danger, so why should I tremble?* (NLT) What's dark and what's light? Shockingly according to the Oxford Dictionary, the meaning of darkness[5] is the *partial or total absence of light.* The synonyms are evil, wickedness, sin, immorality, etc. Light[6] is *the natural agent that stimulates sight and makes things visible.*

Its synonyms are illumination, brightness, shining, glow, etc. Light reveals, exposes, and shows everything.

In 1 John 1:5 we read *This is the message we heard from Jesus and now declare to you: God is light, and there is no darkness in him at all.* (NLT) Because God is light. He is perfect, holy, good, faithful, and true.

Darkness is Satan who is the chief devil, man's adversary, the father of lies, unfaithful to all mankind, evil spirit, deceiver of the universe, and a roaring lion seeking to devour his prey. He traps and tricks people into believing in his waste-of-time schemes and leads precious human beings to sin.

The reason Jesus came was to take our sins away by laying down his perfect sinless life for ours. God accepted Jesus' death in exchange for our freedom. He forgives our sin, and our hearts are restored in relationship with God.

Relationships are getting to know someone not because you have to, but because you have that drive and desire. God is not a religious God; He's all about having a relationship with the people He created. He likes celebrating people and has good and positive thoughts about them. According to Psalm 103:13, *The Lord is like a father to his children, tender and compassionate to those who fear him.* (NLT) Just as your parents are to you, or you are to your own children, He is a father to his sons and daughters.

Honoring and obeying our parents are God's commands, the same way honoring and obeying God are also His commands. When I hear a small voice that I know is not me, I know to quickly obey. I fear God, meaning I am not focused on pleasing people or winning their approval, but I focus on pleasing God in the actions He's instructed me to do[7]. There are good and abnormal kinds of fear. We may fear spiders, rats, earthquakes, scary movies, or more recently—diseases and pandemics. When these consume us so we can't function, they become abnormal. A good or healthy kind of fear is when we listen and do what God is telling us to do. We develop wisdom when we listen to God's instructions. See Proverbs 1:7 *Fear of the Lord is the foundation of true knowledge, but fools despise wisdom and discipline.* (NLT)

I remember my teenage years when I used to tell my dad "I know Dad. you don't have to tell me. I already know." It turns out I didn't really know. The following scripture explains truth perfectly when we think we know it all because we're proud and unwilling to accept other people's advice. 1 Corinthians 8:2 *Anyone who claims to know all the answers doesn't really know very much.* (NLT)

Pride is the number one destroyer in relationships. It can divide people's hearts. Sometimes when my parents told me to do something, I would raise my chin and refuse to do. It hurt their feelings. They wondered why I acted like that. Pride got in the way! After I became a believer in Christ, I was devastated by my actions because I felt badly about hurting them. The only way we can stop from hurting others and then experiencing regret is to humble ourselves first so others can see Jesus in us.

The devil first exercised pride when he tried to surpass God—he uses it today to hurt people. Jesus is humble, full of mercy and grace to heal, set free, and bless people. As we humble ourselves each day, we grow stronger spiritually and develop Jesus-like characteristics. We can do this by fasting, praying, and reading the Bible. We can receive deliverance and experience refreshing life from the Holy Spirit.

Whenever a leader in a workplace, church, business, group, college, school, or any other setting gives you constructive criticism (correction) on something needing improvement, humble yourself to accept it and obey without any hesitation. It's important to lose our pride. It pleases the spirit of God when we humble our hearts during correction so we grow. If we don't learn these things now, we won't have opportunity to grow from it. People offer advice to help you improve and grow healthy or wise. We might feel offended or rejected when someone critiques or criticizes us, or feel hurt, but trust the process that something good will come out of this. It is to help refine our character.

Here is a good example: Friends that help friends by praying, loving, and encouraging rather than letting them do drugs, get drunk, have sex with anybody, because they care so much for their well-being. It's important we open up our minds as well as our hearts; otherwise we are shutting down golden opportunities to grow. The Lord our God knows us better than we know ourselves. God is a father to the fatherless and motherless. He is a genuine God who is full of unconditional love, rare peace, and hard to find joy.

God is good to every single human being. He has so much love for us that He wants to bless us and give us good life. The truth in God's word speaks it. There is no other god or human being that can give us what we ask God to give. Matthew 7:7 says, *Ask and it will be given to you; seek and you will find; knock and the door will be opened to you.*

In this world there is darkness because Satan rules this world. We are so used to living in our culture where it's *okay* to wear clothes that are tight and show our half-naked bodies, where it's *okay* to curse at anybody, it's *okay* to lust after a man or woman, it's *okay* to watch horror, adult, and violent movies, it's *okay* to watch porn because it feels good, it's *okay* to disrespect to our parents, it's *okay* to have sex before marriage, it's *okay* to hold a grudge against someone. For God these things are *not* okay. It may feel, look, and smell good, but the consequences of sin are *not* good. God will not bless your sins. Giving into temporary pleasure = eternal torture. Things that corrupt, kill, steal, and destroy us can enter our hearts and affect how we live making us ill in the future. Our world is full of chaos because of *our* hearts. Christianity is a heart-checker; revealing yourself on the inside instead of what we look like on the outside.

One Father's Day I gave my dad a jumbo card with a monkey on the front and sticky notes naming some of his good qualities. He asked "So I'm a monkey now?"

I responded "It's the inside that counts, not what you look like Dad." I saw qualities nobody ever shared with him, because all they saw was the opposite.

We see people based on what they look like, but we don't know what kind of person they are until we get to know their heart. You know the saying *Beauty is skin deep*. Beauty is within us—not what others see on the outside. Often, we see others based on their looks and don't really know what the person is thinking or feeling on the inside. Beauty is not what you look like, but what your heart looks like.

Don't get me wrong, we all want to look good, but we *need* to check our hearts daily. It's okay to wear makeup to look good on the outside, but if our hearts are far from God and we don't reach out to Him, then our faces will look good while our hearts look ugly. God searches our hearts. I remember asking God to "Search my heart and take out anything that is not of You." In Psalm 139:23 King David pleads with God *Search me, O God and know my heart, test me and know my anxious thoughts. Point out anything in me that offends you, and lead me along the path of everlasting life.* (NLT) God did a work in me by opening my eyes to see what areas needed to be changed. I gave up my pride, lust, sadness, misery, religion, and rebellion.

Matthew 15:18 tells us *But what comes out of the mouth proceeds from the heart, and this defiles a person. For out of the heart come evil thoughts, murder, adultery, sexual immorality, theft, false witness, slander. These are what defile a person. But to eat with unwashed hands does not defile anyone.* (ESV) Your eyes, ears, and mouth are like doors—anything can enter whether it's good or bad. What you see, read, hear, and say is what enters your mind, heart, and soul.

The Holy Spirit works in us and makes us different on the inside. 2 Corinthians 4:16 says *That is why we never give up. Though our bodies are dying, our spirits are being renewed every day.* (NLT) Physically when you eat and chew on a garden salad, you're eating food that is agreeing with all systems of your body. God doesn't just want us to have a healthy body but to have healthy thoughts, words, actions, and motives as well.

According to Jeremiah 17:9 *The heart is deceitful above all things, and desperately sick; who can understand it?* (ESV) Only the Lord knows our hearts because he designed us and knows us intimately. What we see, hear, touch, and say affects not only our minds but also our hearts. What we say to or about people comes from our hearts—good or bad things. Guard your heart according to the Bible verse Proverbs 4:23 *Above all else, guard your heart, for everything you do flows from it.* Protecting your heart from things that can easily enter in is vital. Never let your guard down and keep your head up at all times—with humility.

What are you feeding your mind and heart today? Is it healthy or unhealthy? The mind can be a battlefield. We have negative and positive thoughts each day. If we continue to dwell on the negative thoughts, eventually they may become strong enough that we become trapped in a negative cycle.

We can be free by allowing God to renew our thought life simply by asking the Holy Spirit. He can detoxify our old habits and old patterns of thinking. When we instead dwell on positive thoughts, especially what God has said in the Bible, we experience that freedom.

# JESUS = Everything

There's a song by Kari Jobe[8] that says *If I have you, I have everything, but without you, I have nothing.* The *you* she refers to is Jesus.

When you're making a sandwich, you need bread. Bread is the main food needed daily in our life. If you're missing bread, then your life is incomplete. You're hungry and need it. You don't feel full when you're empty inside.

It works the same way spiritually. Once you have Jesus who is the bread of life, you develop a hunger for more of him. With Jesus, you have all you need in your life—you're whole and satisfied. What you taste, eat, and hear is feeding the inside of you. When we read, chew, and digest God's word from the Bible, it is the bread that gives life and medicine for healing to our bodies, minds, hearts, and soul. It's important that we know what we are putting inside our bodies spiritually and physically to be healthy. We can start by meditating on the word of God every day.

According to Philippians 4:8 we're told to *"Fix your thoughts on what is true, and honorable, and right, and pure, and lovely, and admirable. Think about things that are excellent and worthy of praise."* (NLT) The more we think about something, the more it consumes us. If I were to think about Jesus over and over again, it would bring me joy. If I were to think about someone who said something hurtful, it would break my heart. It can turn into either a pure or impure cycle in my mind. We have control over our minds in what we choose to think about. God gives us options to choose. Let's choose purity, freedom, love, honor, and true things. He created you out of love. Talk to God and let Him know how you feel. Think about that act of kindness somebody did for you. Count your blessings.

After accepting Jesus, I started listening more to worship and praise music, watching Christian movies and television shows, and reading Christian books. After finding Jesus, I lost all interest in clubbing, partying, drinking, watching horror movies, worshipping Hindu gods, and taking various medications. I was growing out of old things and into doing new things. God took away all the darkness I was in and brought me into *His* wonderful light. Why? To set me free and deliver me from the chains that were holding me down.

As a Hindu I would pursue relationships, feeling like I needed them to complete me. I was desperate for love! As a Christian it's the opposite—because of God I am made whole and don't need someone to fill or satisfy my heart. When God knows our needs, He understands and feels our hearts. Only He can provide, heal, and fill our hearts with *His* love. His perfect love casts out fear. The One, who created our hearts, is the One who knows our hearts. Matthew 14:36 says the crowds followed Jesus *And besought him that they might only touch the hem of his garment: and as many as touched were made perfectly whole.* (KJV) A touch from Jesus can make us forget all our issues, problems, struggles, worries, and messes. He can make us whole—nothing lost, and nothing missing, nothing broken.

Truth hurts those who don't believe. But when you believe you'll know and understand who, what, why, when, where, and how. God loves His creation so much that according to the Bible verse Jeremiah 31:3 *The Lord appeared to him from afar, saying, "I have loved you with an everlasting love; therefore I have drawn you with my lovingkindness."* (NASB) No matter how near or far God seems, He *loves* you—no matter what you go through in life. He doesn't like your sin, but *He* loves *You*.

God doesn't want the sacrifices of animals—He has accepted the sacrifice of blood Jesus spilled on the cross. We don't have to keep shedding the blood of animals, when Jesus died one time for eternity. According to Hebrews 9:11-14 . . . *Christ has now become the High Priest over all the good things that have come. He has entered that greater, more perfect Tabernacle in heaven, which was not made by human hands and is not part of this created world. With his own blood—**not the blood of goats and calves**—he entered the most Holy Place once for all time and secured our redemption forever.* (NLT, emphasis mine.)

Under the old system, the blood of goats and bulls and the ashes of a heifer could cleanse people's bodies from ceremonial impurity. Just think how much more the blood of Christ will purify our consciences from sinful deeds so we can worship the living God. For by the power of the eternal Spirit, Christ offered himself to God as a perfect sacrifice for our sins. The blood of Jesus heals *all* diseases, illnesses, and sickness. There's nothing Jesus can't heal, because Jesus is greater than every kind of disease known. He will heal every type of disease from A to Z—you name it, He'll do it. There's power in his blood and his name.

The following table[9] shows the differences between animal sacrifices and the blood of Jesus.

| **Animal Blood Sacrifice** | **Jesus Blood Sacrifice** |
|---|---|
| • Religions today sacrifice the animals to sprinkle blood on themselves<br>• Takes many animal sacrifices for forgiveness<br>• Temporary covering of forgiveness of sins | • Jesus shed His blood on the cross to give us a permanent relationship with God<br>• One sacrifice for forgiveness of many sins<br>• Past, present and future permanent sins are permanently forgiven |

The blood of Jesus is so powerful that it has the ability to heal, restore, deliver, and cleanse every sickness and disease. You can't find His blood at the pharmacy or in your medicine cabinet. You can't buy or sell it. It's not given from another god. You can only receive it by confessing with your mouth and asking God's spiritual power to come into your heart to cleanse you. The choice is really yours.

We have one father who is our Heavenly Father from above. If you want a relationship with Jesus Christ today, there's still time before Jesus returns for his people. Please seek for yourself the joyous presence of God the Father, God the Son and God the Holy Spirit. You can experience *joy* as found in John 15:11 *These things I have spoken to you so that My joy may be in you, and that your joy may be made full.* (NASB) God promises *joy* that He wants to give to all people.

2 Corinthians 7:10 says *For the kind of sorrow God wants us to experience leads us away from sin and results in salvation.*

*There's no regret for that kind of sorrow. But worldly sorrow, which lacks repentance, results in spiritual death.* (NLT) How far or how close are you to God? Close to God means obedience, trusting, believing, and depending on Jesus in everything. Far from God means living in sin that can end up in eternal death. I don't know about you but reading this scripture about spiritual death and being far from God makes me want to give up my dark past.

# ⚜ CHAPTER 3 ⚜

# Identity in Jesus

ave you ever seen the Snickers commercial where one guy says to the other, "You're not you when you're hungry!" Well spiritually speaking, you are not *you* when you're hungry for Jesus. The definition of identity[10] is "condition or character as to who a person is or what a thing is; the qualities, beliefs, etc., that distinguish or identify a person or thing."

The world we live in labels people based on how they look, how they sound, what they say, and what they do. I have been bullied by friends saying hurtful things that I thought was normal. When I didn't know the God of Christianity, Hinduism made me someone I was not meant to be. I always thought it was *normal* to lust, be fearful, be miserable, have a bad attitude and be consumed with worry. To me, that was normal life as a Hindu. I was a slave to these things and wasn't set free until I accepted Jesus in my life. I used to struggle with people telling me things that were not true about myself. I went through life thinking this is who I am because of what he or she is telling me or what they think about me. After going through the process of discipleship, counseling, and mentoring, I saw things from a different perspective.

God loves us and knows who we can become in Christ Jesus. Knowing your identity in Christ is more important than the labels you hear from people. It's what God says about you rather than what people say.

Romans 12:2 states *Don't copy the behavior and customs of this world, but let God transform you into a new person by changing the way you think. Then you will learn to know God's will for you, which is good and pleasing and perfect.* (NLT) God will change the way you think, how you react to different situations, what your response will be in difficult situations, how you say things to people, and what you say to them. Whatever we think about we become. The more we think negatively, the more our actions will be negative. The more we think positively, the more our actions will become positive. Our thoughts lead to our actions.

As I was growing up, there were times where I copied my cousins, dad, mom, friends—almost every single member of my family. I wanted to look like them, act like them, talk like them, eat like them, sound like them—pretty much do everything like them. It was almost like I wanted to steal their identity and didn't care about my own personality or character traits.

I never liked anything about myself. I was insecure in my self-image. I would see a lot of fans in concerts going crazy over a celebrity. I followed the crowd being crazy over them. I wanted to be just like those celebrities. I was a *huge* fan trying to be *like* them.

When we care and know what God says about who we are, we change and want to become more like God. We are not God at all, but we speak words that come from Him, act more like Him, think positively like Him, become bold like Him, and most importantly *love* more like Him. Why do we do these things? The love God gave us is the same love we can give to other people—whether we know them or not. We can show God's love to them because we have that true love living inside of us. Being secure in who you are means you are confident in who God says you are to Him.

The truth is our identity is found in Jesus. We can become more and more like Jesus, and less and less like people and the things of this world. I once was lost, but now I'm found! I was lost in who I was in my religion as a Hindu *but* found who I was as a Christian in my relationship with Jesus Christ.

After Christ, I realized that one thing seemed to be missing from these celebrities, and that is God. The celebrity's life is all about fame, popularity, cars, money, fixing every feature on your face, body surgeries, and the number of shoes and purses in your closet. After Christ I started to realize I don't want to live that kind of life. Because I gave (surrendered) my life to Jesus Christ, I became a changed person. I saw I needed more of the fullness of Jesus and less of the things of this world, because the desires I had in the world no longer pleased my five senses (taste, sight, touch, smell, and sound). Psalm 34:8 says to *Taste and see that the Lord is good . . .*

When you receive the power of God in you, you start to lose your desire for the things this world offers like alcohol, bars, clubbing, addictions, etc. Giving your soul to the Lord instead of to the world is the least popular message you'll hear, but the best choice you'll ever make is to follow Him. There is wealth living inside of me, the Holy Spirit makes me rich in love with God. Everyone can get wild about a person such as a celebrity, but Christians, believers of Christ, are crazy about Jesus because of the fire of love God put in them. God calls His people, those He set free from sin, to tell people who are still slaves to sin about the grace, mercy, and love He has for them.

Sometimes God reveals something specific about what another person might be feeling, thinking, or experiencing. He might even reveal a word of encouragement for them that should be shared. At one point when I witnessed this happen, I became jealous because God spoke through someone else and not me. I felt jealous and angry toward God. Why wasn't God using me that way? I felt hurt for a long time. I was operating out of my flesh and out of an orphan spirit. An orphan spirit is a spirit that tells you lies such as God doesn't accept you, love you, need you, or wants you. God's DNA test says that is a lie! God accepts, cares, loves, needs and wants *us*. It's not God creating the division, it's the devil spreading the seed of lies to destroy and separate people from God.

Whenever you have feelings of rejection, fear, worry, or anxiety, write them down and say over each one, out loud, "I break-off and turn away from all fear, anxiety, worry, and rejection." Write anything in which you know you're struggling. Cross items off as you read through the list, as if you're putting them on the cross, leaving them there, and letting them go so you can be free from them.

Ask God to forgive you for these things, to heal you from any hurt, and then repent—as in *change* so you don't do it again. Trade worry with trusting God, choose to love instead of hate, choose acceptance as a replacement for rejection, and choose to be humble instead of prideful. Walk in freedom and experience a new change—declaring encouraging thoughts every day over and over again to yourself. Trust God, because it's needed. Speak *life* into yourself!

Turn away from the labels people place on you into what God says about you:

From:     Pride to humility
          Negative thoughts to a restored mind
          Hate for people to love for people
          Lust to God's love
          Unforgiving people to forgiving people
          Fear to faith

According to the Oxford dictionary the definition of surrender[11] is: *cease resistance to an enemy or opponent and submit to their authority.* Surrender does not mean be a doormat or be controlled. It's liberation from control. It's letting God take over with His good control. The more we openly tell God everything that's deep within our hearts, for example offense, fear, worry, anger, hurt, wounds, misery, the more God sets us free from things we can't fix on our own. Tell God every day, "I surrender my heart, mind, body, and soul to you Lord," Surrendering leads to freedom from life's daily frustrations, annoyances, irritability, worries, stressors, anxieties, anger, resentment, or _____. (Complete the sentence naming anything else that troubles you.) You can tell that devil, "I'VE HAD ENOUGH! I surrender to God because He gives me FREEDOM!" According to God's word in James 4:7 *Submit yourselves therefore to God. Resist the devil, and he will* ***flee*** *from you.* (NASB, emphasis mine.)

# Surrender to God = Freedom

The world will tell you who you are when you are living in the darkness. God exposes the darkness with His light by revealing who you are in Jesus Christ. Being like someone else, wearing cool clothes, our good efforts, deeds, IQ, performance, titles, appearances, the number of college degrees or what possessions we own is *not* the definition of who we are. Who we are is our gift from God.

God doesn't see our position, our titles at work or school, or how well we do. He sees Jesus Christ in you, and that pleases Him. God is our Father and we are His sons and daughters. When God created you, He didn't create ten, twenty, fifty, or one hundred of you—He created only one of you. Look in the mirror and check yourself out, embracing the features God created in you.

Romans 12:2 starts with *Don't copy the behavior and customs of this world.* It is saying don't copy how people behave or act in the world. Instead of following what everybody else is doing, follow God in conducting yourself differently from the crowd. Holy Spirit can and will renew your mind and heart and can *transform* you. You'll be on your best behavior ever when you have the living God inside of you. God will never lead you wrong; He will lead you toward the *right* direction. We just need to trust Him even when we don't understand.

When we accept Jesus Christ as our Savior, and the Holy Spirit lives in us, God doesn't see us, He sees Jesus in us. He doesn't see our worldly identities—He sees our identity in Jesus Christ. According to 2 Corinthians 5:17 *Therefore, if anyone is in Christ, the new creation has come: The old has gone, the new is here!* Because Holy Spirit lives in us, he changes our hearts and puts in us a new heart of love, joy, peace, patience, kindness, goodness, faithfulness, and gentleness. We are made new from the Holy Spirit.

Before I came to In the Light Philadelphia, I was fragile and hurt by the wounds of my past. I was struggling with many things: fears, worries, anxieties, offense, condemnation, lust, relationship issues, rebellion against my parents, fornication, anger, unforgiveness, pride, etc. I discovered my identity in Christ when I started going to church, witnessing God's light at In the Light Ministries in Philadelphia. Because of God's real presence, I started going to church every Sunday and Wednesday. I would *not* miss a day. I was hungry for God and wanted more of His real *presence.*

I was baptized on September 22, 2013. I will never forget that day because it represented the best decision I ever made. I surrendered my life to Jesus Christ. I became a new person in Christ, and that showed after baptism. Giving my life to Jesus gave me freedom from darkness. God began many changes in my life, providing freedom from things I never thought I would get out of. The changes were not quick; it was a slow beautiful process with God taking away things that were not okay with Him. I moved out for the first time, got out of a dead-end relationship, and began working a new job.

After my baptism, even though changes happened physically, other changes were made spiritually. Let me explain: We have a spirit, body, and a soul. The spirit is where God breathed His life-giving spirit in our bodies. Genesis 2:7 *Then the Lord God formed a man from the dust of the ground and breathed into his nostrils the breath of life, and the man became a living being.* It is the spiritual heart, where God's spirit and therefore His presence dwell. It is the place of the conscience—the voice of His spirit—that convicts us of what is evil and wrong and affirms to us what is right and good.

The body is what we see daily in the mirror. God created the body as a way for our spirits and souls to express themselves and as a means for us to govern the creation over which He has placed us as stewards.

The soul is our mind, will, and emotions. There are a lot of things we carry within our souls that need to be removed daily such as old habits, old mindsets, doing whatever we want to do, and doing what our feelings are telling us to do. It is where we need to receive deliverance—the mind, will. and emotions. Our will (our selfish living) must be surrendered, the mind renewed, and the emotions healed every day.

Reading God's word can transform our soul, mind and body. Hebrews 4:12 says *For the word of God is living and powerful and sharper than any two-edged sword, piercing even to the division of soul and spirit, and of joints and marrow, and is a discerner of the thoughts and intents of the heart.* (NKJV)

Getting baptized in water is not the same as getting baptized in the Holy Spirit. Getting immersed in water is physical. Getting baptized in the Holy Spirit means to be reborn spiritually. We must first humble ourselves, knowing we have sinned against God and need to turn away from destructive wrong doings. Our decision to receive Christ and repent of our sin makes us a new creature in Christ. God gives us the gift of the Holy Spirit. A pastor or any believer can baptize a person in water. Baptism doesn't remove physical debris from the body. It is a sign of our commitment to God and the body of Christ, announcing to others the cleansing of our sins. We make a declaration to the public announcing our faith in Jesus Christ.

God can help us escape from daily sins in which we are stuck, such as the negative thoughts we have, disobedience, and dishonoring our leaders or parents, or road rage against other drivers. We are not perfect since we are human, but we can become more and more like Jesus who is perfect.

Colossians 3:3-4 states *For you died to this life, and your real life is hidden with Christ in God. And when Christ, who is your life, is revealed to the whole world, you will share in all his glory.* (NLT) The life I lived before is dead to worldly desires, and the life I live now is the new life with Jesus Christ because God has forgiven all my sins. Only Jesus set me free from my wounded past. I thank God for setting me free from all the sins I had committed. If I hadn't accepted Jesus, I wouldn't have a relationship with God, and most of all I wouldn't have known who I am in Jesus Christ. I am forever grateful and thankful to my mighty Lord. The following table explains some differences between life before and after Christ.

## According to the Bible[12]

| Before Christ | After Christ |
|---|---|
| Dead because of sin | Made alive with Christ |
| Under God's anger and judgement | Shown God's mercy and given salvation |
| Follow the ways of the world | Stand for Christ and truth |
| God's enemies | God's children |

| Enslaved to the devil | Free in Christ to love, serve, and sit with him |
|---|---|
| Followed our evil thoughts and desires | Raised up with Christ to glory |

While I was serving in a ministry at church I was highly encouraged by my brothers and sisters through the Spirit of God. They spoke over me things that were true from God: honest, lovable, humble, embracing, nice, sweet, willing, happy, friendly, unique, caring, joyful and submissive. I heard the truth about myself instead of the lies and labels people used to describe me. As brothers and sisters of Jesus Christ, we build up one another through words of encouragement, words that will happen in the future (prophetic), and knowledge about who the person is to God. The Holy Spirit that lives *in* us tells us encouraging things about others that are truthful in Christ. We are to share those messages with them. God doesn't see our miseries, our mistakes, our sins, our failures because He sees perfection—He sees Jesus in us.

According to the Bible the following are several things God says about us when we accept Jesus Christ into our lives.

# Our True Identity in Christ[13]

**We are:**

## Declared righteous

Romans 3:24 *Yet God, in his grace, freely makes us right in his sight. He did this through Christ Jesus when he freed us from the penalty for our sins.* (NLT)

## Pure and holy

1 Corinthians 1:30 *God has united you with Christ Jesus. For our benefit God made him to be wisdom itself. Christ made us right with God; he made us pure and holy, and he freed us from sin.* (NLT)

## Set free from the power of sin that leads to death

Romans 8:2 *And because you belong to him, the power of the life-giving Spirit has freed you from the power of sin that leads to death.* (NLT)

## Made right with God

2 Corinthians 5:21 *For God made Christ, who never sinned, to be the offering for our sin, so that we could be made right with God through Christ.* (NLT)

## His masterpiece

Ephesians 2:10 *For we are God's masterpiece. He has created us anew in Christ Jesus, so we can do the good things he planned for us long ago.* (NLT)

## God's possession by the Holy Spirit

Ephesians 1:13 *And now you Gentiles have also heard the truth, the Good News that God saves you. And when you believed in Christ, he identified you as his own by giving you the Holy Spirit, whom he promised long ago.* (NLT)

## Adopted as God's children

Ephesians 1:5, 6 *God decided in advance to adopt us into his own family by bringing us to himself through Jesus Christ. This is what he wanted to do, and it gave him great pleasure. So we praise God for the glorious grace he has poured out on us who belong to his dear Son.* (NLT)

## One in Christ with other believers

Galatians 3:28 *There is no longer Jew or Gentile, slave or free, male and female. For you are all one in Christ Jesus.* (NLT)

## Submitted to Christ's authority

Ephesians 1:10, 11 *And this is the plan: At the right time he will bring everything together under the authority of Christ—everything in heaven and on earth. Furthermore, because we are united with Christ, we received an inheritance from God, for he chose us in advance, and he makes everything workout according to his plan.* (NLT)

## Permanently freed from our sin

Colossians 2:11 *When you came to Christ, you were "circumcised," but not by a physical procedure. Christ performed a spiritual circumcision—the cutting away of your sinful nature.* (NLT)

## Promised blessings

Ephesians 3:6 *And this is God's plan: Both Gentiles and Jews who believe the Good News share equally in the riches inherited by God's children. Both are part of the same body, and both enjoy the promise of blessings because they belong to Christ Jesus.* (NLT)

## Able to boldly and humbly approach God's presence

Ephesians 3:12 *Because of Christ and our faith in him, we can now come boldly and confidently into God's presence.* (NLT)

Declare and take authority everyday remembering who you are in Jesus Christ! All the above is proven true by verses written in the Bible. It's not based on human facts, opinions, scientific discovery, philosophies, or the dictionary. Instead, it is based on what God says about you. Everything God says is valuable, important, and genuine truth. Truth is *So if the Son sets you free, you will be free indeed* according to John 8:36.

# Submission to God[14]

James 4:7-8 *Submit yourselves, then, to God. Resist the devil and he will flee from you. Come near to God and he will come near to you.*" How can we experience the love of God?

1. **Submit to God.** Let God take over your mind, heart, body, and soul by trusting, listening, and obeying what He says and directs you to do. Let go of your control and know God is the ruler of your life, if you allow him to be. Follow His ways.

2. **Resist the devil.** Don't listen to the lies, thoughts, and temptations he provides. Don't have any conversations with the devil. He creates unnecessary chaos leading to destruction. Stay away from wrong doings of any kind.

3. **Wash your hands and purify your heart.** Our hands were created for destruction or construction. When we use our hands, we can point fingers to people, steal from stores, or cook a good meal for someone, touch products, buy things for people out of love, or use a pen or a pencil to study hard for exams pursuing the career to which we are called. We can also use our hands to kill people with guns, knives, or other weapons. We depend on our ten-digit hands for everything. Our fingers can be used to like pictures on social media that either agree with the Lord or agree with the devil. Our hearts are connected with our fingers because what our heart says is what our fingers do. We are cleansed by our actions and saying *no* to sin. Crave and stick to wanting a pure heart and mind.

4. **Grieve, mourn, and wail.** If you sin, admit and confess it to God. Sin is sin—no matter how big or small it is, it is still sin. When you confess your sins to God, you will feel refreshed. Don't be afraid to confess it to God, because He will forgive you no matter what kind of sin it is. Confession exposes the devil's deeds.

5. **Humble yourself.** Instead of telling God, *I got this* (Mr. or Ms. Independent), tell God, *You've got this!* We live in this world where being prideful is okay. When God told me to pray for someone and I didn't do it, I basically ignored Him and thought I knew better. That is pride. When He told me to pray for someone, and I chose to listen and take action, I was humble and obedient to Him. Choose to be humble to God. He will bring you supernatural (what you can't see because it is in the spiritual realm) favor.

I highly encourage you to find a local church so that *you* can also experience the presence of God's love. It's a presence not to be missed. Before selecting a church, first talk to God and ask Him to lead you to the right church where He wants you to attend. God will direct you there if you ask. If you don't have a church available, you can still invite the Holy Spirit to come to wherever you are— whether it be in your bedroom, at school, at work, or in your car. His presence will come near you if you allow and ask him. It will happen if you believe!

## ❧ CHAPTER 4 ❧

# Spiritual Armor

Accordingt to Amazingfacts.com[15] it is estimated more than fourteen thousand, five hundred wars have been fought from 3600 BC to present day—and that number keeps rising. In fact, during the same time period, there have been five thousand, three hundred and five years of war … and only two hundred ninety-two years of peace. Jesus talks about wars in Matthew 24:6, 7 *You will hear of wars and rumors of wars, but see to it that you are not alarmed. Such things must happen, but the end is still to come.* Jesus knew this was going to happen.

We are currently undergoing a constant war of physical and spiritual battles. We see this in the news twenty-four hours a day, seven days a week. Jesus and Satan are in constant battle for our hearts, souls, and minds. Your body is in a state of war between the flesh and the spirit.

Flesh[16] means our physical bodies, souls, and minds without the power of God. We are empty spiritually without Him. John 3:6 states *That which is born of the flesh is flesh [the physical is merely physical], and that which is born of the Spirit is spirit.*

(AMP) According to scripture in Galatians 5:19-21 *The acts of the flesh are obvious: sexual immorality, impurity and debauchery; idolatry and witchcraft; hatred, discord, jealousy, fits of rage, selfish ambition, dissensions, factions and envy; drunkenness, orgies and the like.* When you follow your flesh, it leads to self-chaos, violence, wars, prisons, clubs, bars, pornography, murder, suicide, cheating, rebellion, disobedience, witchcraft and many other things that are common in this world.

In Galatians 5:22-23 we see the opposite, *But the Holy Spirit produces this kind of fruit in our lives: love, joy, peace, patience, kindness, goodness, faithfulness, gentleness, and self-control. There is no law against these things!* When you follow what the Holy Spirit tells you, he leads you to run around, and jump up and down with joy. He gives you inner peace, a big smile on your face, and constant laughter. The Holy Spirit gives blessings, overflowing love for one another, serves people with love, builds and lifts people up. With him we help and feed the people that are weak spiritually and weak physically. He gives us patience in different situations such as driving on the road, waiting in line whether it be at the grocery stores, a restaurant, drive-thru, etc. Fill in the blank with areas in which you need patience: _____.

Holy Spirit prompts us to do many more acts of kindness such as paying for someone's food, helping with their groceries, bringing flowers to your teacher or boss, or leaving a generous tip for the waiter. Have you ever touched someone's heart through your acts of kindness? Have you ever given or done acts of kindness so excessive you might touch someone's heart by "killing them with kindness?"

According to Ephesians 6:10-17 *A final word: Be strong in the Lord and in his mighty power:*

*Put on all of God's armor so that you will be able
to stand firm against all strategies of the devil.
For we are not fighting against flesh-and-blood
enemies, but against evil rulers and authorities
of the unseen world, against mighty powers in
this dark world, and against evil spirits in the
heavenly places.*

*Therefore, put on every piece of God's armor
so you will be able to resist the enemy in the time
of evil. Then after the battle you will still be
standing firm. Stand your ground, putting on
the belt of truth and the body armor of God's
righteousness. For shoes, put on the peace that
comes from the Good News so that you will be
fully prepared. In addition to all of these, hold
up the shield of faith to stop the fiery arrows of
the devil. Put on salvation as your helmet, and
take the sword of the Spirit, which is the word
of God.* (NLT)

Each piece of armor is designed for a purpose. It is used in
battle against the enemy, Satan. He is our worst enemy. God
gave us full armor to equip us for both protection and battle.
Just like a police officer or a military solider, a warrior would
wear the proper armor and have their weapons ready to come
against any threat to protect people. Spiritually we wear full
body armor daily to protect our mind, heart, and ears from
the lies of the devil, and instead defeat him by using the word
of God as our weapon.

Look at the following table to see how each item provides
peace when in war!

*Anjli Sharma*

# God's Armor[17]

| Piece of Armor | Purpose of Item |
|---|---|
| **Helmet of Salvation** | To be free from negative thoughts, words, mindsets, ideas and opinions |
| **Body Armor of Righteousness** | To guard your heart—the core where our feelings, emotions, and trust lie |
| **Belt of Truth** | To buckle your waist with God's truth instead of Satan's lies |
| **Sandals of peace to spread the Good News** | To walk anywhere and everywhere spreading God's word in love, peace and joy. Walking in victory and freedom. |
| **Shield of Faith** | To use for protection from Satan's weapons that brings conflict, temptations, dishonor and problems. |
| **Sword of the Word of God** | To use to pierce the enemy with God's word |

I encourage you to read, know, and declare the spiritual body armor of God over yourself every single day because we live in Satan's world. We are not fighting against people we care about and love, we are fighting against spirits from hell that we *cannot* see or hear behind a person. These spirits cause people to fight against people; they cause arguments, violence, division, and war against one another. That's not what God intended for His people. He didn't create us to go against one another; He created human beings for *love* and not *war!* We don't understand it because we cannot see in the spiritual realm. We ought to be fighting *for* each other instead of *at* each other. We can rebuke and command the demonic spirits pitting one person against another to *leave* in the name of Jesus. 1 Peter 5:8 *Be of sober spirit, be on the alert. Your adversary, the devil, prowls around like a roaring lion, seeking someone to devour.* (NASB) Stay alert at all times because the devil is working overtime and we must guard ourselves with full spiritual armor twenty-four hours a day, seven days a week!

Our best pieces of battle equipment are the Bible and our testimony which are weapons against the enemy. They are considered weapons because the devil does not want us to share our testimony, read our Bible, pray, worship, go to church, or speak in tongues (a heavenly language that communicates to God). The devil knows they go against him and expose him. The word of God exposes the schemes of the enemy. God is light, and His word is light. There is not a single ounce of darkness in God. The light exposes the enemy and tears away the darkness. It is much better being the terrifying threat to the enemy than being in life without Jesus.

When we get a cut on our skin, we immediately put a band-aid on it instead of only applying ointment to it. We cover it up and act like everything's okay. It's like the word of God. When we read the word, we apply it instead of just reading it. We don't need to display a mask when the word of God reveals who we are and opens our hearts to things we didn't know we were struggling with. Hebrews 4:12 teaches us: *For the word of God is alive and powerful. It is sharper than the sharpest two-edged sword, cutting between soul and spirit, between joint and marrow. It exposes our innermost thoughts and desires.* (NLT) It is protection over our minds, hearts, soul, and spirit. The Bible is a weapon against the enemy because it speaks God's truth. Every single word in the Bible comes from God. Think of it like this: the surgeon is God; the tool to cut open and fix the heart is the Bible. God penetrates our moral and spiritual life by cutting us with the Bible. He goes to the deep vein of our hearts and removes anything that destroys us.

2 Timothy 3:16-17 says *All scripture is inspired by God and is useful to teach us what is true and to make us realize what is wrong in our lives. It **corrects** us when we are wrong and **teaches us to do what is right**. God uses it to prepare and equip his people to do every good work.* (NLT, emphasis mine.) It's important to let the Bible shape our lives and also to let Holy Spirit transform our hearts, minds, and bodies completely. You can read the whole Bible and meditate on every word written, but the most important thing is to exercise your faith. It's like when you're at the gym, and you're working out to reach a weight-loss goal, fit into a dress, become healthy, etc. You do something about it by exercising those muscles until they grow bigger and bigger. It's the same with faith; we keep on exercising our spiritual bodies, which increase our faith until we reach the goal of maturity. We get stronger and stronger as we grow in God. And you can do this too! It's not the quantity (number) of years you've walked with Christ. It's

the quality (building character and producing fruit) of your walk with Christ.

This is explained in John 15:1-4 *I am the true grapevine, and my Father is the gardener. He cuts off every branch of mine that doesn't produce fruit, and he prunes the branches that do bear fruit so they will produce even more. You have already been pruned and purified by the message I have given you. Remain in me, and I will remain in you. For a branch cannot produce fruit if it is severed from the vine, and you cannot be fruitful unless you remain in me.* (NLT)

It's a different process for everybody. Not everyone will have the same walk with Jesus. We all function differently in our personality, perspective, character, gifts, talents, etc. When we accept Christ in our lives, it's a process that we go through to come to a place of being ready to align our heart with God's heart. It's beautiful to God to watch our growth. It's like a father seeing his son growing and enjoying his child day by day. We never stop learning and growing spiritually.

The following table tells how to destroy the works of the devil's plans, assignments, tricks, tactics, schemes, ideas, and strategies. It shares different kinds of weapons God gives us to be fully prepared to fight the good fight of faith.

# Weapons of Warfare[18]

**Pray** A.C.T.S- Adore, Confess, Thank, & Supplication. Adore God, Confess to God, Thank God, and bring your requests to God. Pray for others because they need it too— just like you.

Philippians 4:6 *Be anxious for nothing, but in everything by prayer and supplication with thanksgiving let your requests be made known to God.* (NASB)

**Praising and Worshiping** Hallelujah is the highest form of praise. Singing songs and lifting your arms to God brings you freedom. The more you worship, the more you will encounter His presence.

Ephesians 5:19 *Singing psalms and hymns and spirituals songs among yourselves and making music to the Lord in your hearts.* (NLT)

**Fasting** To fast is to sacrifice what is most addictive to you (keeping it on the down-low because it's personal between you and God) and replacing that with prayer and devotion to Him. It pleases God's heart and brings spiritual break-through. Example: Fasting from Social media, TV and/ or junk food.

Matthew 6:18 . . . *so that your fasting will not be noticed by men, but by your Father who is in secret; and your Father who sees in secret will reward you.* (NASB)

**Bible** The Bible teaches, corrects, trains, and gives the devil a black eye when we apply it to our daily lives.

Hebrews 4:12 *For the word of God is alive and powerful. It is sharper than the sharpest two-edged sword, cutting between soul and spirit, between joint and marrow. It exposes our innermost thoughts and desires.* (NLT)

**Name of Jesus** Saying his name many times a day frightens every demon wanting to fight against us.

Romans 10:13 *For "everyone who calls on the name of the Lord will be saved."* (ESV)

**The blood of Jesus** Jesus who died on the cross shed his blood for us. The blood of Jesus has power and high value. It permanently forgives all sin.

Ephesians 1:7 *He is so rich in kindness and grace that he purchased our freedom with the blood of his Son and forgave our sins.* (NLT)

**Our Testimony** Our testimony is a big deal. Sharing your testimony shows you're honoring God and defeating the devil.

Revelation 12:11 *And they have conquered him by the blood of the Lamb and by the word of their testimony, for they loved not their lives even unto death.* (ESV)

**Obedient Life** When God tells you to pray, heal, read a scripture, worship, or even give, then He expects us to obey Him. It is our responsibility to listen and obey God because after obedience comes blessing. It brings us joy. We will reap joy. Obeying God pleases His heart.

Exodus 23:22 *But if you carefully obey his voice and do all that I say, then I will be an enemy to your enemies and an adversary to your adversaries.* (ESV)

**The gift of tongues** It is a heavenly language that communicates with God. When we speak in tongues it gives strength to the Holy Spirit inside of us. It brings alignment of our mind and heart to God. We are connected to God in this way.

1 Corinthians 14:14 *For if I pray in tongues, my spirit is praying, but I don't understand what I am saying.* (NLT)

**Calling** God calls us to be somebody—to do something to change people's lives. He calls us for a reason, a purpose, and a destiny to change history.

Ephesians 4:1-3 *I therefore, a prisoner for the Lord, urge you to walk in a manner worthy of the calling to which you have been called, with all humility and gentleness, with patience, bearing with one another in love, eager to maintain the unity of the Spirit in the bond of peace.* (ESV)

If you were ever hurt, discouraged, broken hearted, couldn't trust, depressed, had any suicidal thoughts, there's good news. *Jesus* will accept you as you *are*. You can give him all of that and he can exchange it with his love, joy, and peace that is real. If you would like to accept Jesus into your heart, I encourage you to pray this prayer:

> *Dear Father,*
>
> *I know that I have broken your laws and my sins have separated me from you. I am truly sorry, and now I want to turn away from my past sinful life, toward you. Please forgive me and help me avoid sinning again. I believe your son, Jesus Christ died for my sins, was resurrected from the dead, is alive, and hears my prayer. I invite Jesus to become the Lord of my life, to rule and reign in my heart from this day forward. Please send your Holy Spirit to help me obey, and to do your will for the rest of my life.*
>
> *In Jesus' name I ask and pray, Amen.*

Here is my prayer for you: *I pray God will give you wisdom and knowledge to speak—for abundant joy, eternal peace, and unconditional love to come into your heart. Let him direct your paths and guide you in your spiritual journey with Jesus Christ. In Jesus' name I ask and pray. Amen!*

## ❧ CHAPTER 5 ❧

# Power of Prayer

The purpose of prayer is to communicate with God—it opens the doors to God's heart. Philippians 4:6 *Don't worry about anything; instead pray about everything. Tell God what you need, and thank him for all he has done.* (NLT) Instead of worrying about what to wear, what to eat, what to do, where to go, what to know, or how to do, we can turn our attention to praying about it. Will you pray about the small, medium and big things that you worry about in your daily life? We can come to God with all our heart, mind, and soul by calling on Jesus. God will answer prayers in Jesus' name because there is power in Jesus' name to do mighty miracles, healings, blessings, provision, and protection.

John 16:23-24 says *At that time you won't need to ask me for anything. I tell you the truth, you will ask the Father directly, and he will grant your request because you use my name. You haven't done this before. Ask, using my name, and you will receive, and you will have abundant joy.* (NLT) In this scripture, it says Father which means God. The words that says, "because you use my name" is referring to Jesus. We can ask God without any shame, guilt, fear, or worry. Will you ask Jesus today?

Mark 11:24 states, *For this reason I am telling you, whatever things you ask for in prayer [in accordance with God's will], believe [with confident trust] that you have received them, and they will be given to you.* (AMP) Believe God can and will answer your prayers. All you need to do is ask. Pray with a strong belief knowing it's going to happen when God brings it at the proper time.

Prayer is the key in building a foundation and it changes people's hearts. The following table presents a strategy to help you know where to start when it comes to praying. There's no set formula on how to pray the right way. The following is simply a tool to help guide you in knowing what to pray and how to pray.

| | |
|---|---|
| **ADORE** | Admiring WHO HE IS. Creator, healer, deliverer, provider, Father to the parentless (no parents), motherless, or fatherless, lover of our souls, and Master of the Universe. |
| **CONFESS** | Humble yourself to God by confessing your sins, faults, mistakes, fears, lies, pride, bitterness, unforgiveness, or anything else that you need to tell God about. Confess. Repent. Renounce the sins. |

| THANKSGIVING | Thank God for every single thing He has done for you: home, spouse, children, job, school, friends, specify exactly what you're thankful for. Cultivate an attitude of gratitude with all seriousness. |
|---|---|
| PRAYER REQUESTS | Pray for God's will to happen in every person's life, unity in people's hearts, cities, nations, people, salvation, freedom from bondage, strongholds, marriages, churches, the world. Pray for a filling of the Holy Spirit of peace, joy, love, gentleness, kindness, humbleness, patience and self-control. Pray for everything God puts in your heart. |

Whether you pray individual prayers or group prayers, prayer closes the doors of demons, darkness, depression, suicide, worries, fears, wars in homes, anger, strongholds, shame, etc. It doesn't matter where you pray, whether it is at a coffee shop, concert, movie, work, school, home, church, gym, park, or museum, you can pray anywhere, anytime at anyplace.

God *will* hear your prayers. We can pray any time of the day, it doesn't matter if it's 6 a.m., 10 p.m., or 3 a.m. We also pray when God asks us to pray for whatever He puts in our heart. We don't run on our own schedule to pray, but His schedule because we are led by the Holy Spirit within us to pray. There were times when God would wake me up in the middle of the night with back pain and I couldn't get up, my body wanted sleep. I discovered God wanted me to get up and pray. It's hard to get up when God wakes you up on His timing, but easy for us when our body exercises its own timing. There is more demonic activity happening at 3 a.m. than 3 p.m. any day, because that's when more people sleep than pray.

When we don't know how to pray about something, we can ask Jesus to help us in our prayers. We can ask His will and ways—not what everybody else wants us to do. When we pray, we position ourselves by bowing our heads, bending our knees, and raising our voices to speak to Him. We pray for Jesus to set us free from the prison of sin. God moves in people's hearts and shifts the atmosphere by His presence. He changes things by bringing bits of heaven down to earth.

Where there is God, there is His light, love and joy to spread contagiously to other people around us—to fill and change the atmosphere. God's presence feeds people with his love, joy, kindness, gentleness, peace, patience, goodness, faithfulness, and self-control. *All* of these things above can produce Christ-like character. Praying for these things makes God happy. Praying for our character to be more like Jesus is more life-transforming than how all the wealth in the world would change us.

You can have one-and-a-half billion dollars with a broken heart, *or* you can have a *rich* soul filled with God's love and be highly blessed and favored. God cares more about your heart than your money. I asked Jesus "Is asking God for a million dollars in God's will?"

He spoke to me and said, "Do you want it for the right or wrong reason? It depends on your heart's motives or intentions." I thought *Wow, that makes sense.*

The heart has impure and pure motives or intentions. If we trust our own heart, we are trusting in impure motives and intentions, which can be sinful. I used to trust in the Hindu statues that never spoke, saw, or heard anything from me. I would feed them when they couldn't open their mouths. When God opened my eyes to see the real truth about idols, I trusted in the Lord Jesus by turning away from worshipping them. I didn't have a relationship with the Hindu gods, only religion. God desires a relationship with His people more than a religious ritual.

In Matthew 6:9-13 Jesus teaches his followers to pray like this: *Our Father in heaven, may your name be kept holy. May your kingdom come soon. May your will be done on earth, as it is in heaven. Give us today the food we need, and forgive us our sins, as we have forgiven those who sin against us. And don't let us yield to temptation, but rescue us from the evil one.* (NLT) Talk to God how you would talk to a friend. For example, when you talk to your friends, you want to know what their interests are—their likes and dislikes. They listen to what you're saying from your heart and mind. That's what it's like when you're being real to God about things you need to talk about. Be honest about yourself to Him. Talk to God about every little thing.

Pray for yourself, people, family, your next-door neighbor, the person across the street, your brother, your cousin, your principal, the president, the rapist, terrorists, and people from different religions. Everybody on this planet needs prayer. God wants us to pray for them, because He loves and has mercy on them.

We may wonder *why would we, why should we pray for someone who is not good to us?* Remember we are not fighting against people—we are fighting against demonic spirits controlling people in the unseen spiritual world. People have broken hearts, and they need Jesus to heal them. God loves the sinner, not their sin. God does hear our prayers even if they're not answered right away, but God can do it. He can make anything happen because *nothing* is impossible for God.

Matthew 6:5-6 instructs us, *And when you pray, you must not be like the hypocrites. For they love to stand and pray in the synagogues and at the street corners, that they may be seen by others. Truly, I say to you, they have received their reward. But when you pray, go into your room and shut the door and pray to your Father who is in secret. And your Father who sees in secret will reward you.* (ESV) Praying on the streets for show, impressing others, or showing off doesn't please God. You've only tried to impress others to secure your outside image. Instead, spend time behind closed doors in that private place where you can be alone with God to worship, pray, and read the Bible.

Jesus is known as the water of life. Our souls crave and hunger for lasting eternal love. When we get near Jesus, His love is like a spring of living water bubbling up inside us. Your heart can be on fire for God because His love has touched you. Get soaked in His presence when your bones are thirsty for God.

Another way you can also pray is by reading scriptures from the Bible. Read Psalm 91:1-16, replacing "you" with "me". *For he will rescue me from every trap and protect me from deadly disease.* Make this your personal prayer to God.

> *Those who live in the shelter of the Most High will find rest in the shadow of the Almighty. This I declare about the Lord: He alone is my refuge, my place of safety; he is my God, and I trust him. For he will rescue you from every trap and protect you from deadly disease. He will cover you with his feathers. He will shelter you with his wings. His faithful promises are your armor and protection. Do not be afraid of the terrors of the night, nor the arrow that flies in the day. Do not dread the disease that stalks in darkness, nor the disaster that strikes at midday. Though a thousand fall at your side, though ten thousand are dying around you, these evils will not touch you. Just open your eyes, and see how the wicked are punished.*
>
> *If you make the Lord your refuge, if you make the Most High your shelter, no evil will conquer you; no plague will come near your home. For he will order his angels to protect you wherever you go. They will hold you up with their hands so you won't even hurt your foot on a stone. You will trample upon lions and cobras; you will crush fierce lions and serpents under your feet!*
>
> *The Lord says, "I will rescue those who love me. I will protect those who trust in my name.*

> *When they call on me, I will answer; I will be*
> *with them in trouble. I will rescue and honor*
> *them. I will reward them with a long life and*
> *give them my salvation."* (NLT)

I would highly encourage you to never stop praying for people who are in need for prayer. Prayer changes people's lives, and shifts the atmosphere in cities, nations, and our world. God answers our prayers when it comes from the Holy Spirit living inside us. When we pray, we pray out of confidence, faith, and trust—knowing and believing God will answer our prayers. Pray out of trust, faith, and belief.

There's a story in the Bible about Jesus healing the blind. According to Matthew 9:27-30, after Jesus left the girl's home, two blind men followed along behind him, shouting, "Son of David, have mercy on us!" They went right into the house where he was staying, and Jesus asked them, "Do you believe I can make you see?" "Yes, Lord," they told him, "we do." Then he touched their eyes and said, "Because of your faith, it will happen." Their eyes were opened, and they could see!

I had a completely blind co-worker whom I asked to pray for, and one year later she said she saw *a tiny light*. There's nothing impossible for God to do.

It's important to trust God no matter your situation. Don't lose hope. Don't be discouraged. Don't give up. Don't grow tired. Don't lose sight of your dreams. Don't worry. Don't doubt. God's got this! Proverbs 3:5 *Trust in the Lord with all your heart; do not depend on your own understanding.* (NLT) Never stop praying.

I am so glad you've chosen to read this book. Remember Jesus truly loves and desires your heart, soul, and mind. It's not too late to accept Jesus as your only Lord and Savior today.

If you would like Jesus to be your Lord and Savior, then you can pray this: *Lord Jesus, I know that I am a sinner, I repent of my sins. Come into my heart and I will make you my Lord and Savior.*

The heavens rejoice after one sinner repents and comes to Jesus. Accepting Jesus is the best decision you could ever make. If Jesus can change my life, He can transform your life too.

Thank You for reading my book!

I really appreciate all of your feedback, and
I love hearing what you have to say.

I need your input to make the next version of
this book and my future books better.

Please leave me an honest review on Amazon letting
me know what you thought of the book. You can go to
Amazon.com and type in *From Hinduism to Christianity*.
Scroll down to the reviews section, and share your
thoughts in the "Write a customer review" box.

THANK YOU!

*Anjli*

# Citations

1   Heidler, Robert D., *Set Yourself Free: A Deliverance Manual* (Denton: Glory of Zion International Ministries, 2010), 41

2   Guillermo Maldonado, *Supernatural Deliverance* (Wheaton, IL: Tyndale House Publishers, 2016), 224-225

3   *Life Application Study Bible Notes*, (Large Print) (Carol Stream: Tyndale House Publishers, 2004), 13

4   https://www.loc.gov/item/lcwaN0003960/

5   https://www.lexico.com/en/definition/darkness

6   https://www.lexico.com/en/definition/light

7   http://lifehopeandtruth.com/god/who-is-god/fear-of-the-lord/

8   "Always Enough" (by Kari Jobe), 2014

9   *Life Application Study Bible Notes*, (Personal size) 2101-2102

10  https://www.dictionary.com/browse/identity

11  https://www.lexico.com/en/definition/surrender

12  *Life Application Study Bible Notes*, 2003

13  Rosa Defeo, In the Light Ministries Church, 2015

14  *Life Application Study Bible Notes*, 2120

15  http://www.amazingfacts.org/media-library/book/e/52/t/the-armor-of-god

16  http://www.gotquestions.org/the-flesh.html

17  *Life Application Study Bible Notes*, 2009

18  Rosa Defeo, In the Light Ministries Church, 2015

www.ingramcontent.com/pod-product-compliance
Lightning Source LLC
Chambersburg PA
CBHW070643030426
42337CB00020B/4141